T0146593

SILENT VOICES
HIDDEN WISDOM

Telepathic Conversations
The Frontier of a New Era in Human Evolution

KAREN KOBER

BALBOA.
PRESS

A DIVISION OF HAY HOUSE

Balboa Press books may be ordered through booksellers or by contacting:

Balboa Press
A Division of Hay House
1663 Liberty Drive
Bloomington, IN 47403
www.balboapress.com
1 (877) 407-4847

Because of the dynamic nature of the Internet, any web addresses or links contained in this book may have changed since publication and may no longer be valid. The views expressed in this work are solely those of the author and do not necessarily reflect the views of the publisher, and the publisher hereby disclaims any responsibility for them.

The author of this book does not dispense medical advice or prescribe the use of any technique as a form of treatment for physical, emotional, or medical problems without the advice of a physician, either directly or indirectly. The intent of the author is only to offer information of a general nature to help you in your quest for emotional and spiritual well-being. In the event you use any of the information in this book for yourself, which is your constitutional right, the author and the publisher assume no responsibility for your actions.

Any people depicted in stock imagery provided by Thinkstock are models, and such images are being used for illustrative purposes only.
Certain stock imagery © Thinkstock.

Print information available on the last page.

ISBN: 978-1-5043-6858-2 (sc)
ISBN: 978-1-5043-6860-5 (hc)
ISBN: 978-1-5043-6859-9 (e)

Library of Congress Control Number: 2017901073

Balboa Press rev. date: 02/28/2017

DEDICATION

W.A. FOXX
1997 - 2010
white/blue-eyed Siberian husky

Who awakened the spirit within me
to know we are limitless.

♥

"I come to you as a spirit in the body of a dog.
We are to begin our journey to walk as One."
-Foxx

MISHA
2004 - 2014
white Temple dove

Incarnate angel who gave each day its song.
A gift from God who arrived with rainbow wings.

♫

A gentle soul who trusted everything larger than her.
Who offered peace to everyone who held her.

Contents

Chapters

Preface

Life followed the usual doldrums of routine. Routine, a safety net, holds boundaries for security. I had always known animals were sentient, though science was giving its thumbs down. A beagle named Snickers showed me his ability to make choices. To make choices is sentient. Snickers learned many tricks. At the end of his tricks, I would ask him to make a choice for one. He never made the same choice. Each session ended differently.

One evening, I sat down to listen to an Internet radio program. The host—a movie star, author, and spiritual person—was interviewing an animal communicator from New York. The week after the radio program, I signed up for a workshop to learn animal communication. I was going to learn to communicate with our dog. During the workshop, a conversation with Foxx changed my life instantly and forever.

Curiosity pulled me forward into the exploration of spirituality. Guidance came from many different directions: ascended masters, spirit guides, family and friends in heaven, and animals. I had to be astute to notice a message when it came in synchronicity, music, someone saying something to me, intuition, or dreams. The list continued.

An elementary teacher told my mother I would never write or publish anything. She stated that my mind raced faster than my hand could write, which resulted in jumbled sentences and paragraphs. She was right.

I had the deep, inner knowing as I grew into adulthood that I would write. Others would be able to comprehend my writing. It was a challenge. The passion to write moved my endeavors forward. Now, in my seventh decade, this has come to fruition in writing articles and three books. This is the first book.

I look back at the years and wonder how I accomplished so much in my life. A little at a time was my only conclusion. I still had one more thing to do. I wanted to be an architect. After a life of learning, I realized that I was done with homework. Was I really done with homework? As I type this at the computer, a new form of homework arises that will expand outward with the hopes and dreams of reaching out to others.

My curiosity is never satiated. The world has expanded and evolved into learning more than any dream could hold. Telepathy was the start, and God had more tasks for me than I thought I could accomplish in one lifetime. He is not finished with me yet!

After years as an international professional telepathic communicator, I have noticed that I no longer need to explain what I do. I no longer hear people saying, "I know what my dog wants when he wags his tail." Do you? Do you know its favorite color, what it dreams, what its individual conversational voice sounds like, and what your animal wants to learn or accomplish? The list is as individual as each animal. Yes, I do hear their individual voices. It is fun talking with a pit bull with a Scottish brogue. Animal interests would bring a joyful laughter. "I'm going to an educational facility" (dog training to learn fly ball). Animals laugh, cry, mourn, and have emotions only thought for humans.

Let me not forget the rest of nature, earth, heaven, and other dimensions. The faeries, unicorns, dragons, elves, and leprechauns are a reality. They can be observed with inner vision and with a digital camera. The last faerie photo I snapped was a faerie hiding under a towel from our cat, Znah Mae. The wind, rain, water, trees, rocks, and all of nature can be heard. These communications bring their viewpoint of observing history, inspiration, and wisdom. Telepathically speaking, the universe translates their voices into English. Therefore, a dog living in China who has only heard the Chinese language is easy to talk with.

The following pages contain what the animals—in their infinite wisdom—wanted to give you. The insights were channeled from above and within. Life holds no secrets. Telepathy will change our world. Lies, nasty comments, stealing, rape, murder, and negativity will be known by everyone. The web of life binds us as One.

Therefore, kindness and compassion will prevail. Love is a given; honor and respect are higher. There cannot be love without honor and respect. Telepathic communication with intention is a new era in human evolution.

I have read and reread what the animals have offered. I find the depth of what they say goes deeper and deeper. I wrote down what the animals and spirits said. I am only a repeater; that is my job. Their joyful words and insights allow moments to pause, ponder, and inspire.

"The path has been,
Long for the two-legged,
Their spirit has faded.
To seek spirit,
The earth provides,
The sky provides.
Dance the circle,
Dance the four winds,
Follow the trail,
Spirit returns."
—Turquoise, stone

Chapter 1

All is Well

Stop! Take three deep breaths. Inhale the presence of the Creator through your nose. Hold it, exhale through slightly pursed lips, and release any negativity from within. Drop your shoulders to release the muscle tension accumulated throughout the day. Close your eyes and know that everything is all right. Sense an inner peace within.

See yourself interacting with an individual or a group of people who surround your existence in this life. Maybe it is a child, an animal, or someone at work—just anyone or any situation that has pushed you to the limit. You love them, yet your buttons have been pushed by their behavior.

Life gives us pushes and shoves—often not in the nicest way. Our bodies tense, and our breathing changes into shallow respirations. Take a moment to breathe and find the quiet place within. Stress is like a very cold day: we hold the body more stiffly, and the chills become worse. Relax and feel warm. What are you observing? Why is the behavior of others demanding your attention? What are they seeking from you?

There is a choice to respond with compassion, being aware not to provide incentive for more inappropriate behavior or attention seeking. The behavior will stop when one turns heel and walks away, not allowing an interaction and providing the audience they seek. Turning away eliminates secondary gain. Secondary gain is the personal reward for attention. Children will learn to quiet themselves. As parents, we provide safe environments to allow children to resolve their issues. Pushing buttons for attention will stop when they do not receive it. The way we respond is always our choice.

This is the everyday stuff that life is made of. What about encounters with people who approach with negative or evil intents? They make it known that our presence has no meaning for them. They have no consciousness of right versus wrong and no inner feelings of guilt or remorse.

The observation of behavior holds no judgment. Our responses hold no judgment. We are aware that those people will always be on earth. They appear empty, ignorant, arrogant, or hollow. Their auras are brown, gray, black, or absent. We are not responsible for them. It is their journey—and their journey alone. Silently bless them, be pleasant, and move away quickly without future contact. Become aware of the list of sociopathic symptoms, and keep vigil for them because they will enter our lives. They present with charismatic personalities cloaked with negative intentions. Develop awareness of disruptive, manipulative, and dangerous personalities. These negative indications will provide information about when to walk away. This is a protective measure for personal safety and family safety.

Patience is a gift to us. Life is also full of people who lift our spirits. It is serene to encounter these people with positive souls. Their light radiates joy and compassion. Experiencing the joyfulness, kindness, and compassion people emit makes living life worthwhile. We are entering into the Law of Grace, responding in kindness, and leaving behind the Law of Karma, which says what goes round comes round from our negative behavior. We progress into living life in kindness with the Second Coming. We will encounter more and more people with the Christ consciousness awakened within them.

Join the celebration of a new beginning of interaction grounded in unending love. Aspire to enjoy the freedom of being and giving joy in each moment. Life becomes fun with giggles. It is simple to start the day by rolling on the floor to initiate laughter each morning, and we may find our giggles turn into healthy roars of laughter. This moment (and every moment) is ours for creating the world around us.

Mirror

There are mirror reflections of our souls,
Of our attitude,
Of our kindness,
Of our patience,
Of our compassion,
Of our integrity,
Of our joy or sadness,
Of our creativity.
It matters not what we impart;
It matters what others see in us.
When looking into our being,
They are the mirrors of our reflections.

Chapter 2

Rambling

Is there a beginning and an end? A front and a back? What is between the sandwich? What is in between? There is a middle to everything. It is not yesterday or tomorrow—and it is not what holds things together. It is the moment of life when we consciously navigate our thoughts, awareness, observations, and perceptions. Yes, it is the concentrated and in-between thoughts. It is also those darned rambling thoughts—those incessant thoughts that interject themselves without permission. Who gave that song permission to loop through my mind all day?

We seek to have quietness between the rambling thoughts. We ponder if it is truly possible to be in sincere solitude without these thoughts. The ego tells us it is not possible because it wants control. I remind the ego it is to be in service to humans. Two plus two is four. Yet it hangs on like sticky gum on the bottom of a shoe. Again and again, I remind the ego it has its time and place in my universe called life.

Can I make those thoughts that are not pertinent in my life restrain themselves? Yes—but only if I constantly remind myself they are not important and release them. The enjoyment of daydreaming, meditation, and drifting off to sleep are a few of those moments. Daydreaming is pleasant—to disassociate into the pleasant and calming visual beauty in life, to lose oneself in the eyes of a baby, to become one in the beauty that surrounds us and is in us. The connection to God in meditation is blissful. His words encompass all. His love is always present, lulling us slowly into slumber, making us feel safe, and letting us know everything is all right.

Music that is rambling its notes or lyrics through our minds over and over or grating our nerves with a mechanical sound is irritating. There is the opportunity to choose music that provides serenity. The sound of God is found in music that is 440 Hz. We feel this in Beethoven's "Pastorale Symphony," composed in 1807; "Amazing Grace" (original composer unknown but written in the late 1700s), published by John Newton in 1779; and "Silent Night," composed by Joseph Mohr in 1616 with lyrics written by Franz Xaver Gruber in 1818. There are many more sounds of music in 440 Hz that embrace us into the silence of just being, just listening. Music created in 440 Hz holds the vibration of God, and it is God. Our souls connect with it, and we inwardly know there is something beyond us where we belong. The music holds us frozen in the moment where nothing else exists.

These moments of pure peacefulness are fleeting. In our yearning to recapture peace, we are able to slow our respirations and heartbeats, and we can relax all our muscles—to just let go and let God.

Karen Kober

"Now is the time to begin a new love
And share it with the world.
Now is the moment to share a new joy
And share it with those loved.
Now is the truth to impart new strength
And share it with compassion.
Now is the future to release new sight
And share it with a new insight.
Now is the life to sing a new song
And share it with all the earth."
—Suki Yaki, cat

Chapter 3

Beats and Breath

Lub-dub, the first heartbeat of a new creation in the womb. The first cry of deliverance fills the lungs with air. A steady pulse and respirations are the miracles within our soul-body. These continue in miraculous strength for the entirety of our time in the physical world. They will sustain our physical forms until they both cease for the return to the eternal. What is not lost in our cessation is our consciousness of eternal awareness.

The moment spirit enters the soul-body is undetermined, though many have sought the truth. Some imply it is in the fetal stage—others at birth or during the next few months. We have all witnessed the alert newborn and others in vagueness. The spirit determines the timing of its arrival. The spirit comes in with an abundance of knowledge—knowledge of life's very beginning with our Mother and Father God, our eternal wisdom, all our past lives with family and friends, and knowledge acquired through the soul's interplay with us to learn our experiences on this playground we call earth.

What does this spirit seek between the first and last breaths of life? The challenges agreed upon in our heavenly written script for spiritual expression. Yes, we can imbue slight choices in living our scripts. Overall, our scripts are sealed contracts with God that proceed to completion. Free will is the choice to live this earthly life in God's will or away from it. The positive and productive choice is to live life as a child of God.

Joy is the abundance of love in the present moment. We can also moan and choose to live in fear. Joy and fear cannot reside in the same space—it becomes a choice. The exuberant choice is joy! Our Lord Sananda said, "One is giving love when one brings joy. How do you do this? By being joy, radiating joy, and expressing joy. Joy is expressed in smiles and laughter. Is there joy in sadness or sorrow? Yes! For joy brings hope and peace."

Where may we find our wisdom of choice? Within the body, there are two hearts! The sacred heart, which is also called the divine heart or zero point (the point where we begin, conceptualized as a black hole), sits behind the physical heart where God resides within us. It is a sacred space deep within our souls. In this space, all questions are answered.

We are given guidance and direction because the all-knowing God is within our divine hearts. The divine heart is the wisdom of the universal oneness and is each individual's inner journey into oneness. An inner realization is the joy in knowing we are not alone and never were alone.

We are able to reach this divine heart during meditation, an ancient discipline. The answer lies within this space, and there is the fruit of love. Prayer is talking to God. Meditation is listening to Him. Communion with God (prayer and meditation combined) is holding the scared conversation reverently executed in silence. Silence provides the privacy in communion with the Divine Oneness. In silence, this experience is surrounded by a tunnel or light beam directly to God; no other entity in all dimensions may listen to this communion. Who could hear? All can hear when not given in silence to receive its protection.

How do I acquire this communion with God? This space is entered without expectation of the outcome. Those moments are experienced in the loss of awareness of surroundings, holding focus, or intention. It is the feeling of daydreaming. It is the present moment of joy and serenity when one is focused on one thing—gardening, hiking, creating artwork, channeling, pondering, sighing, or any moment that drifts you away. There is no time or space element involved. Our surroundings fade away when we are focused.

Communion with God is constant and eternally present. To enter this sacred space, notice your heart beating or your breath rhythmically moving your chest up and down. Even the sounds of your beating heart or rhythmic respirations fade away into oblivion. You are becoming one with the Creator.

In the etheric, our spirits profusely announce our eternal quests for perfection. As seekers of perfection in human form, we are reminded that God has created all in perfection. He only knows His creations as perfection. We are perfection in His image. We know what perfection looks like when we look upon our reflections, the reflections of others, and the reflections of creation. Perfection is total love for God and compassion for all His creation. In Him we are created into the eternal light of His wisdom and love.

"Gentle, soft, and silent are my paws,
Gentle, soft, and silent my love purrs.
Gentle, soft, and silent are my prayers,
Gentle, soft, and silent my heart purrs."
—Rosie, cat

"My soul is linked to my friend,
My heart swirled love without end.
I am here to help my friend,
His time is near without end.
I shall fly him home my friend,
In heaven there's love without end."
—Znah Mae, cat

Chapter 4

Birthing

Birthing is giving rise to a new beginning, a new idea, and starting again. To birth is the end of something that no longer exists. The conception and the birth of a child give life to another spirit. Spirituality and expansion of oneself may offer a new beginning or birthing of each moment.

The phrase *higher self* has perplexed me. Do I really have a higher self? Do the angel on one shoulder and the devil on the other create the choice of conscious living of what works and what does not work? Is it the mystic origin of our beginning as created by Yeshua for His Father? He created my spirit and expanded it into physical form. My eternal spirit name is Cherise. Yeshua's first physical life was as Amelius. The Bible called Him, Adam.

My eternal name, Cherise, is exactly that for all eternity. Eternity is beyond my scope of comprehension. How many zeros does eternity contain? What is the power number? In this life, my parents named me Karen. I respond to both names since Cherise still exists within and around me. I do not know if anyone has figured out exactly where our true spirits really reside, and yet connected to each of us in an unknown space.

On earth or in heaven, my spirit is always Cherise. On earth, I have had many names for each life lived. My spirit enters each new life on earth, or another planet, and is given another name to hold dear. The soul is the physical self or personality that we recognize in our current and past lives. The cycle continues for eternity as the choice to return into a physical form.

Yeshua says, "We are like a book with many chapters." Yeshua uses the term *re-manifestation.* Re-manifestation is the desire to experience ourselves in other lives. Each re-manifestation is part of the journey to understand who we are, what we are here to learn, and to grow spiritually. In the journey of re-manifestation, we remember our etheric lives in the eternal aspects of us. We do not die! We transform from physical into spirit and back again in eternal circular motion. This eternal journey creates a sacred circle of our corporeal self and our heavenly self.

Cherise is the eternal, spirit form of me. Karen is the soul and physical form of me. Our souls are our personalities and our lives here on earth. It is who we are in physical form. Our souls are the physical experiences of our journeys in life. We have numerous physical souls—each with their own individual experiences. They are present during our lifetimes in different souls that are experiencing different times, ages, and places. It may seem complex. I could be an adult female in America in 2016, a newborn baby boy in Africa in 1964, and an elderly male Eskimo preparing for his transition in 1898. They can all be concurrent in time and space. Our spirit forms encompass all of our physical souls.

Ghosts are beings that do not transition to home/heaven and remain in the midst of this world. People may remain in ghost form due to unexpected or traumatic deaths, unfinished business, the desire not to leave what they feel is theirs, or for revenge. There are several types of ghosts, including those who are residual, repeating a certain period of time unaware. There are those who see us, hear us, and interact with us in conversation (sentient). True spirits have crossed over into heaven and return to visit us, guide us, or help us. We recreate this journey many times to help ourselves and others grow spiritually.

Where is heaven? It is here among us in another dimension, yet it is separated from us by a *veil.* To see or communicate across the veil is to use one's Holy eye or telepathy. The veil has thinned. In the future, everyone will see and hear through the thinning veil. The veil has thinned twice since the Dawning of Aquarius. We will see, talk, and visit again with family and friends in heaven. There will be a direct hotline to heaven!

Spirit is everywhere and in everything. It is easy to converse with all spirits. Everything is sentient: the wind, a tree, a rock, an animal, and all that is created by God. We are connected by a conscious particle that vibrates and is connected to everyone and everything in this universe. This particle is God. Yeshua calls this the "adamantine particle"; science uses the term God or infinite particle.

The expansion we experience is not linear. It occurs in the oneness—all at the same time. I am born, youthful, adult, and elderly. I am experiencing many lives in many locations all at once. How do I know about these past, present, and future lives? Man has created the time-space continuum, and in this continuum, we are able to trace the other lives we are experiencing simultaneously.

A phylum of angels writes a record in every moment of what we think, say, create, and do. These documentations are kept in a library in heaven called the *Akashic records*. The Akashic records hold our past, present, and future experiences. We can access these records through journeying, hypnosis, meditation, or psychic readings.

Our expansion into knowing is difficult to understand at first because our egos do not want us to know. How do we know this is true? The truth is in our divine hearts, which are behind our physical hearts. It is also called the zero point within us from which we are created. It is a sacred place to go to during meditation. Great answers are found there. We seek the truth by going within our Divine Heart, or God spaces.

Belief is a word that holds doubt in its meaning. Belief usually comes from a third party or institution that wants you to incorporate what they believe rather than honoring the Creator's truth within you. Belief reflects the term *brainwashing*. One will believe what a parent or an institution believes. It causes separation and division.

We are giving birth to something all the time: ideas, innovative concepts, and new cells within our bodies. We are birthing our creations. Where do our thoughts come from? I used to think my creative thoughts came from me. Then I awakened and acknowledged that these thoughts and choices were given to me by family and friends in heaven, angels, spiritual guides, or God. After this realization, I knew that I could not take credit for them. I gratefully thanked them for the gift. Inspiration comes from divine guidance.

13

A simple, powerful prayer is just two words: "Thank you." These two words are frequently used in heartfelt gratitude and have a continuous awareness of blessing, yet it is especially wonderful to say this two-word prayer when you wake and before you fall asleep. Have gratitude for each breath to love Him and what is in front of you now.

I told someone special that I was in his heart next to God—and he could find me there. He did not understand and asked what I meant. Why find me there? That is where love is. I am him, and he is me. This is the recognition of ourselves in others and all of creation. How do we show it to others? The Bible says, "Doing unto others as you would have them do unto you." (Matthew 7:12).

Love is a given; without honor and respect, there cannot be love. Love is the expression of God. The three words interchangeable to represent God are Love, Life, and Light. They have many names and yet no name. I asked Foxx what they call Mother and Father God in heaven? He replied, "Jovena and Jehovah."

Awareness is the awakening of the spiritual being within each of us. If one holds doubt, one will eventually know here, in heaven, or in a future life. An atheist believes in God. In order to deny him, one must acknowledge his existence.

To give birth is being as God created us and to have all the answers of truth within us. It is the light, and this is how the term *light worker* came into being. We work spiritually in the radiant light of the God within us compassionately with all life. We experience life in the light of his/her love. You are in my heart next to God. You are me. I am you. We walk not separately—only as one, mingled in the elements of the universe.

"Diamonds are the sparks of life,
Rubies are the blood of life,
Sapphires are the water of life,
Emeralds are the seeds of life.
Diamonds, rubies, sapphires,
And emeralds,
Gems of the earth,
Blessed by the stars."
—Ruby, bay horse

Chapter 5

Color and Music

Blessings, miracles, surprises, chuckles, and tears? Let's take a screeching halt here. Yes, there is an abundance of blessings to be grateful for—more than one can count. Two that are not often mentioned are sight and sound. Color and sound play important roles in our lives. They are inspirational and change our emotions.

We use color and music to make choices throughout the day. Both color and sound impact our lives in many ways on a subconscious level. Did you reach for that yellow dress or red necktie this morning—or was it the blue one? You may have chosen without even a thought. Was it a feeling—or did it express itself subconsciously? Could it have been an angel or spirit guide that helped guide you to this color? Was this color meant to help you through something today? Was the color of the box at the supermarket designed to help you to choose which product to purchase?

Colors give us many feelings—passion, hunger, peace, happiness, calmness, and anger—and many emotional responses. What instilled us to paint that room hot pink? A little red on a business card designed in teal will draw business. Color comes into fashion, cars, and home decor years before it is shown on the market. There is an abundance of research into colors and its effects upon people.

Animals have preferences for colors too. They see colors around people to determine what is happening with them or whether they are safe to be with. They see a green glow of color around a food source to know if it is safe to eat. If no color is present, they will not eat it. Their paw prints leave a green glowing color on the earth for months, and they can follow those paw prints back to a person or a home. The green glow appears like snapped Halloween sticks. Animals live with the abilities that God instilled in them, and it is natural for them. They have no fear when using them. Humans are unaware or deny their abilities.

I asked our Siberian husky, Foxx, what his favorite color was. He replied, "Yellow." Yellow? I am not impressed with the color yellow. Months later, I awoke one morning and realized our bedroom was painted a colonial yellow. For Foxx, yellow meant being with family, sharing the bed, and sometimes sitting up all night to protect us from what we visually could not see. Yellow meant family and love to him.

When I offer myself as a vehicle for healing from God to a person or animal, the healing modality I use is called *holographic healing*. In my Holy eye, the lungs may be the color blue, the spinal column orange, the pancreas red, and so forth. The organs appear bright as if there is a flood light inside them. The disease shows as black spots in this bright color. I reach into the body with my hand ethereally (to use our holy eye to view the hand moving into the physical body), which is a shamanic way to remove the black (diseased) areas. Why is it this way? I have no idea; it just is.

Seeing these areas in color with the Holy eye is a blessing for those who seek God's healing because it is only He who heals. This healing has expanded into a new modality of spiritual healing; nothing remains stagnant in place or time. It was foretold this would happen, and it did. The result was a miraculous healing.

Each individual organ in our bodies emits a specific sound wave. When an organ is diseased, the correct vibration of sound is given to change the frequency back to the normal vibration for this particular organ—and healing results. We use tuning forks to check the status of our chakras. We hum and whistle tunes to give ourselves comfort. I once observed a wonderful, well-known healer using clicking and whistling sounds in his process for healing others. He said he did not know where it came from. He had always done it that way. He had instinctively known how and when to do it since childhood.

In heaven, there is a special place of healing and rest. Some call it a hospital, yet it is not as we know a hospital to be. There is an empty, low-lit, gray room for healing that is filtered with a specific color mist. It is like the wispy smoke emitted from an incense stick. The color present is the specific color we need for individual healing. It is very calming, euphoric, and peaceful in the room of color healing.

Music reaches our souls via vibrations that change our moods or help us heal. Music can be heard and impact us subliminally. Before starting college, I had a summer job as a waitperson. I worked in a popular restaurant where a music program changed specific music and tempos during certain times of the day. It was a product designed to move the flow of employees and business. When the restaurant had its busiest times, it played the theme song from the *Lone Ranger* (the William Tell Overture composed by Gioachino Rossini in 1829). I waited and watched for the customers' reactions to the music. The customers could not get their forks to their mouths, missed their mouths entirely, or dropped their food. The effect was interesting. It was very, very funny. It did move the crowd to a faster pace of eating their meals and leaving sooner. When the music ended, the next selection was peaceful and calming. The booth was made ready for the next waiting customers.

We grow up not knowing why certain colors and music influence us. At times, music filters in a time warp of nostalgia from a certain point in our lives. I am sure the songs that were popular during my time in the womb gave way to yearning and aching to hear them again and again throughout my life. The old songs were like comfort food that harkened back to an earlier time of feeling safe, secure, warm, and cuddled. We find ourselves reflecting back on these times when the music plays or we hear Grandma making Christmas cookies. For me, it was the childhood memory of hearing the same music playing on the radio at the bus depot while I enjoyed an egg salad sandwich, a chocolate malt, and banana cream pie. Comfort food for the soul is tied to the memories of youth or being in love. It is a moment that inspires the memories of times our souls wish to recreate and relive without the intention of doing so.

We express someone else's feelings with descriptions of color: red for anger, blue for sadness or depression, green for envy, yellow for joy, brown for down in the dumps, and black for grief. Our friend, Alan, saw each day visually in a different color upon awakening. I am sure it impacted his life on a daily basis. A few years after his death, I mentioned it to his sister. She did not know he could do that. She said she was the same way. Seeing each day in a different color speaks of a strong spiritual life.

A memory from my childhood was the sound of church bells filling the air on Sunday mornings. Some chimed hymns. Each of the town's church bells followed in sequence for the morning call to worship. The four churches that rang their bells in timed sequence were Catholic, Lutheran, Congregational, and Methodist.

Lost are the sounds of bells for the call to church, the proclamation of a wedding, or Christmas Eve worship. The complaints of a few ended the bell ringing because they wanted to sleep longer on Sunday mornings. I deeply miss the bells and the organ music flowing through the church doorway on Sundays. For centuries, bells played a role in life. My yearning to hear those bells, which harkened the sharing of faith, has faded in time, yet not in my heart.

Taps played fills the silent air of a cemetery, and every note sears the soul for the loss of life and the sound of tearful mourning. The sound has sadness and despair wrapped in grief. Taps gives honor and shows respect for departed soldiers or veterans. In those moments, we wish it were never played. General Daniel Butterfield and a bugler, Private Oliver Wilcox Norton, composed Taps in July 1862.

Color and music, when joined as one, offer complete harmony, unity, and a total sense of well-being. Together, they offer balance in our lives and connect us to the universe. Color and music have inspired greatness and creativity in people. Composers and artists fill our souls with inspirational beauty. Our innermost beings are reflected in the color and music of our choices.

Our personalities change in the presence or lack of color and music. We worry about children who color only in brown and black or who show distress in the coloring of their lives on paper.

The music of life and the sight of color in nature, sunshine, or clouds bring a rainbow of dreams to my day and I hope in yours.

Karen Kober

"Lord holds me in His Love,
I seek repose in heaven above.
Wonders are infinity where,
Miracles are born.
Shooting stars are messages,
From heaven torn.
Lord has me in His arms,
I seek repose in heaven above.
I seek comfort in heaven above,
I know, I know, I am his love.
Shooting stars are messages,
From heaven torn."
—Sassafras Black, Siberian husky

Chapter 6

Dazed

My heart sank, and teardrops silently coursed down my cheeks. A furry creature that had come bounding into our lives many years ago, sustaining us through the trials of daily life, was in the end stage of his life. The love given to us was more than unconditional; it was sacred. It may sound unreasonable and contradictory, but it was more than absolute. Love came in its purest form.

Our white, blue-eyed Siberian husky was named W. A. Foxx. His love was always present in his wise guidance of my soul. The words guide and dance combine to form the word guidance. He has guided me, and we have danced in the stars.

"What is the purpose of animals on earth with humans?", I asked. Foxx replied, "Humans need us. They have forgotten what their true spirits are. We come to help in whatever way is needed. We live physically, but our spirits soar into other realities or realms beyond earth or dimensions. We help the seen and unseen."

I know you have shown me that you can show yourself in spirit whenever you so choose. How often I have said to you that I did not see you there—only to be met with the response from you that I didn't need to.

We have journeyed together in spirit into the unseen as I slept. My mind remembers nothing in the morning. I sleep the sleep of the ruby red slippers. A tornado could take me away, and I would not know it. When I asked you what we did you said, 'We always help people first. Last night, we crossed six people into heaven to their awaiting family and friends. We went to another star system and danced. Then we—"

Hold it! I interrupted his rendering of our experience. It rang loud and clear in my soul that I understood my journey with Foxx. I know why I am so exhausted at times. It is from astral travel with Foxx the night before. The exhaustion is unbearable as I struggle to move one foot at a time throughout the day. Next time, I will prepare for a slow day before our spirits soar into the night.

I am asked how I hear you. People and psychics often think I am doing a reading. This is so far from the truth. You have taught me that the spirit is the being that I am conversing with whatever the form—human, animal, tree, water, and more. All are intelligent, sentient beings. A spirit exists within the form of a physical body in the living and in the etheric body of the nonliving. The soul body has intelligence, yet the spirit knows all.

You know more about me than I do. You arranged the universe to come into my life, and you found me again. Once you were our red and white, moon-faced, blued-eye Siberian husky named Candy. I am aware of only these two husky lives you have had with me. This time, you told me of our journey together, already knowing what it would be. Your words are deep in the soul of my heart since we have journeyed as One. You tell me we have experienced all my lives together except the first one.

You guided me to learn how to hear the animals and were extremely excited with pure joy when I did learn. You patiently waited for my spirituality to grow so that I could understand the fullness of your knowledge and wisdom. You have loved me beyond my deepest dreams fulfilled. You have looked sadly and compassionately upon me as I cried and nuzzled my tears away. Your joy is present when we see each other and when we sit together on the front porch to idle time away. Your eyes twinkle, and your spirit glows with love. You spin around, pound your paws, howl, and hug me with fervor. You dance and rejoice in exaltation when I do spiritual work to help others.

You are gentle in your love for all. You have special, gentle tenderness for babies and children. You are forever ready to help with your healing abilities for people or animals. People and animals I have spoken with lovingly find you present at their sides when they are ready to cross into spirits. Your presence with them gives their families comfort in knowing you are with their loved ones in the special moments of their departure and unlimited grief.

Foxx is powerful beyond words and comprehension. I told him, "You are the prayer in my heartbeat." I saw the pooling of tears in your eyes looking into mine. My eyes tearfully pooled in response. You said, "No one has ever said that to me before." Our moment of shared silence and love will be in our hearts forever. You truly are the prayer in my heartbeat.

People ask me if their animal wants euthanasia and if it is time? I often hear from animals that their human companions wait too long to give the final graceful assistance for their journeys home. They wait for the daze of death to appear and for the animal's eyes to glaze over into a death-like empty vagueness. Animals tell me that, at that point, it is long past time. The suffering is unbearable. They wanted to cross over sooner, yet they were often held back by their companion's grief, frozen in their inability to release them. Let go or when God says enough—I am bringing you home.

I understand a few animals request no help at all. They do not want to have others watch in curiosity. I have great difficulty with this. With compassion, we are releasing a spirit from excruciating pain. Death does not often come quickly, and this time of endurance must be horrendous. Euthanasia is merciful. Maybe we have offered euthanasia in selfishness to relieve our pain by releasing the animals in pain? Our hearts ache at the thought of emptiness of separation. In truth, the animal's message to their guardians is: "Thank you. I love you. There is no guilt in euthanasia. There is only love. Give the love you gave me to another; now you honor and respect the life we shared."

Some animals prepare for their spiritual departures from earth by sending out a telepathic announcement to people the animal wishes to say good-bye to. These are the bell ringers—people you have not seen in months who come to share time with the animal they have known. No one told them; they just came and rang the doorbell. An animal may wait for a family member to return home so they may have their last moment with them to say good-bye.

There are occasions where animals run away to find seclusion. Death is between them and God—without witnesses. The earth cradles their bodies and gives energy for their journeys home. Their bodies are left to nourish others in the cycle of life, which offers honor to those who partake. I understand the choice to die in nature—to honor and nourish another animal.

Some have special requests: a favorite blanket, a toy, or a person to be with them when they depart. Animals tell me that acceptance of death was the way it was meant to be. They send their messages of gratitude to be free of pain and suffering. Release from a declining, painful body brings a wonderful feeling of freedom and wholeness in spirit form. They say a thank you for releasing them and extend their love to their guardians.

Death is a beautiful release into spirit. In your simple words of "Ho-hum, in body and out of body, no big deal," I try not to ponder if I will have the strength when it is your turn. We both know I will offer and do what needs to be done because I love you. I love you deeply—beyond the simplest empty words I could use to inadequately describe the unspoken bond between us. Love, as you have taught me, is not hanging onto a body that is no longer you. It is letting go, but it is never good-bye. Your presence in spirit will be felt, and I will hear your words until you return to my life as the same spirit in a different body.

My soul has a deep longing to hug you forever. I want to look into your eyes as we share my pillow with your head next to mine. It is a comfort to feel your heartbeat and your body rise and fall with each breath. I want to feel the warmth of your fur as you lay next to me. I want to hear the sound of your "hewoa" (hello) "wuv u" (love you) as you proudly form the sounds of speech. We sing our special song together; as you sing to God, I hear the wolf sounds in your melody. The way you intently listen to me stirs my heart.

You and the other animals have taught me that a prolonged period of grief or guilt dishonors our relationship. I can honor our love by loving another and welcoming this new family member into my life with the abundance of love that you and I shared. Love is a given. Honor and respect are high above love. There cannot be love without honor and respect. You have respected and honored me in the twinkling dance of your eyes when you see me. There is no way to hold back my smile when I see you and the exuberant joy that radiates from your presence.

Animals are the teachers of life, joy, love, patience, compassion, death, and re-manifestation. Most creatures have shorter life spans than humans. They teach us that death is not final—and it is not who we are. We are eternal in God's love. I will carry your words with me: "Ho-hum, in body and out of body, no big deal."

Foxx says he has been with me before in all my past lives except the first. He will be with me again and again until I spiritually no longer need to be in the physical body. He views himself as a wolf. Foxx sings his praises to God, his soul and spirit resonate with greatness.

You have taught me about the universe and about God. You tell me you have so much more to teach me. I am eager to learn. I walk with you as One and carry you in my heart always. Do not be gone long—I beg you.

I know you will return, and we will share life together. I know you will come for me when it is my time, and this will comfort me in those moments of not being able to hold you. I know you will come, and I will not fly alone. You will be at my side.

You are out there in spirit helping others. I received your card about the meaning of our life together. I receive calls from people that have seen your spirit and tell me how you helped them, their families, or their animals. Many people have called to tell me their animals were with you when you flew home. I saved the sympathy cards for you to read. They were placed on your memorial table. I know you read them because they were meant for you. Until then, my heart cries—and my tears flow as I await your return. Being human at times gets in the way of remembering the truth.

Foxx asked for euthanasia, and we made the call to the vet. He said he could not hang on to the age of fourteen. He said it was time to go because evil was moving into our home. He said we should leave. I made an impression of his paw and told him it was to show he walked this earth. I could feel the pride he felt with those simple words.

He was peaceful that morning as he looked at the paw print and smiled. His peace gave me comfort as I watched him standing by the window with the sun shining upon his face, knowing he would be free to fly home in a few minutes. He seemed to be contemplating his life here and all the things he needed to do when he returned home to heaven.

He wanted a white candle to be burning and his head to face southwest toward the Apache nation. I drummed, and Henry sang a shaman song and held him as he took his last breath on August 9, 2010. His spirit will be back in a new physical body. He says I will find him. He says that when I find him, I will know it is him. I trust his wisdom.

Foxx, you cajole me when I cry by saying that I have the box (your ashes). Yes, I know you are not there in the box. You are here next to me.

"Thy Father, thy Lord,
I am humble in your heart,
Your light shines in me, around me,
By day, by night.
I sing praises to thee,
For in thee is thy might,
Lo and behold, we are One,
By day, by night."
—W.A. Foxx, Siberian husky

Chapter 7

Desire and Dreams

We desire, dream, and design our wishes to have goals to fulfill our lives. One yearns to know what our lives will be in youth, adulthood, and aged years. We are constantly seeking our inner reflections in life and how we express them in our lifestyles, partners, homes, careers, and creative designs.

We passionately express who we are through our families, our jobs, our interests, and how we present ourselves. We give compassion to others to express our inner selves. Is it true to who we are? Do we create façades of what we want others to know about us? The truth frees us from our perceptions when we accept what or who is in front of us.

The simplest aspiration to project who we are announces to the world that we are okay and you are okay. Take a sigh and think of three positive things about each person before speaking to them. This opens the awareness that each being we encounter is God's creation, a reflection of ourselves.

Desires and dreams design our realities and accomplishments from moment to moment. Seeking the best we have to offer ourselves, others, and this world is comforting and brings awareness that we can change the world in any given moment. Choices come to us constantly if not instantly. Do I want the vanilla or the pecan ice cream? Is one greater than the other? Is it a choice or a preference? Nothing is greater than another; it just is.

Do we stumble at times? Absolutely! Does life pull punches? Absolutely! All it means is that we can make other choices and create change. If we are unable to create change in the things we observe, then we must change our attitudes about them from within. We error as humans, but we dust ourselves off and move forward again with the desire to make another choice. We create choices because each moment life gives us the opportunity to choose. This is simple, right? How or what would you prefer in any given situation?

February has three days marked for enthusiasm: Groundhog Day, Valentine's Day, and Leap Day. These days express our desires and dreams for an early spring, warmer weather, and the change from snowflakes into flower petals. February 14 is an opportunity to express our love for our partners, families, and friends. We honor who they are in our lives. Every four years, there is an extra day in February for love. This is a gift from the universe.

The joy is greater when we express our love for the Creator and creation. Do you ask God how He/She is doing when initiating a prayer? Some people say, "I want," "I want," and "I want it now." The prayer of gratitude and wisdom connects us with love. Prayer is talking with God, and meditation is listening to God for guidance. The powerful two words—I AM—in our every breath creates the hope that we will live life fully and securely in God's will. Trusting God requires faith. We know that we are living our written scripts and seeking the truth of our personal relationships with Him/Her.

Desire is a beautiful word. It means that we yearn, aspire, and crave to be the best we can be in any given moment, knowing what we have to offer others and creation. There is not a day that exists in our lives when desire is absent. I hope that your life is fulfilled and celebrated in greatness of love.

"Stretching out long and smooth,
Curled to slumber as I snooze,
Romeo is my name; life is but a game.
Run with tail up, balancing my way,
Skid with paws to stop, braking away,
Romeo is my name; life is but a game."
—Romeo, cat

Chapter 8

Eternal Stars

Let me not stand at your final resting place and weep with the sadness of missing you. I know I can no longer hug you, kiss you, hold you, sit by you, or hold your hand. Your touch eludes me, yet it embraces me.

I miss our small talks, big talks, funny talks and long talks. I miss our understandings and misunderstandings. I miss the expression in your eyes and face from joy, sadness, smiles, tears, compassion, hopes, and dreams. My dreams are filled with your physical movement as you passed through life. Standing, walking, running, and making gestures were part of your flow. The activity of the world held your attention. Your thoughts and queries about the world offered insights. You remembered instantly and spoke the names of people from years past. It was a gift. They inspired you, and you moved them forward to create passion in their lives.

The little joys and big joys of watching the world of heartbeats brought smiles and funnies to your thoughts. The antics of animals melted your heart, turned up the corners of your mouth, and brought merriment to your eyes.

The front door no longer opens, and the back door no longer shuts with the sound of your hand on the doorknob. The floor no longer holds the sound of your footsteps. The rocker no longer creaks as you nod off to sleep. The clock key is no longer inserted, and the clock no longer chimes since it was only set by you. The water that showered you is silent, and the fragrance of you is lost. The bed is quiet without your snores. Your musical instruments no longer play their notes with your breath between. The moments of sound heard in silence are no longer here with me.

I no longer stand at your resting place and sigh in sadness because you are not there. Your total love watches over me. You visit me in the wee hours of the night. In my dreams, you whisper of love in my ear. I am at peace and comforted by sensing you near. There is only happiness because I know you are always here with me—sight unseen.

Your last gift to me was the greatest gift you ever gave me. It was a rainbow of memories to fill the rest of my years. I feel abundant joy in knowing you will take my hand and lead me home to God and heaven. We will embrace our love throughout eternity—among the twinkling, eternal stars and God's love for us.

"Wise is my soul that sheds the light to others,
Powerful is my soul that embraces you,
Graceful is my soul when it honors you in me,
Hope is my soul moving forward in the snow,
Peace is my soul finding comfort in creation,
Love is my soul sharing the holiness of us."
—BoJangles Banjo, Siberian husky

"Red, orange, yellow, green,
Blue, indigo, and purple seen,
Colors, colors everywhere.
Fields, streams, clouds sheen,
Valleys, meadows, grasses green,
Colors, colors everywhere."
—Isis, Rottweiler

Chapter 9

Fish

Fish—millions of fish and thousands of species—are in the ocean. Some are alone in constant motion, searching the ocean in an endless quest for survival. Some hide in sand, rock crevices, and caves, waiting for something smaller to appear. They strike out at their food as it swims by.

Some wait for another fish to be enticed or haphazardly cross their paths, drawn in by a harmless behavior that has evolved in their physical being for survival. Some are camouflaged, hidden in their surroundings, and are not noticed by the aggressive and vulnerable. Some are hidden in the depths of darkness and emit internal lights to show the way or give deception as to who or where they are. Some swim in schools, feeling the safety of numbers against becoming prey.

All fish—large, small, transparent, or microscopic—are constantly seeking minute-to-minute survival. Alone or together, each one is a part of the food chain. Each life feeds upon the life force of another. This is labeled in our world as natural.

A thick piece of glass holds a huge room filled with water that is landscaped to recreate a stream, river, pond, or sea. It's a façade of life—whether it is a small fishbowl, an aquarium, or an outdoor holding tank.

At an aquarium in New Jersey, the fish were doing the same things they did in my grandma's aquarium. They were swimming together in tandem and turning in the same sequence in the slightest fraction of a second. In an instant, they changed direction as one unit: one direction and then another in an endless ebb and flow, a wave of silent and serene fluid motion.

Many small fishes grouped together to appear like one large fish. A large school of small fish, camouflaged by their vast numbers, flowed together in unity to hide from becoming eaten. I asked an aquarium staff person why and how they knew when to turn as one unit. Apparently, no one knew the answer.

The answer was simple and not complicated in the slightest. There is a soul leader, and the leader telepathically sends the message to guide the others in the next movement. Telepathy is thought transference from one being to another. Does it work to move as one? In this large mass of small fish, the bigger fish took their bites for survival. The mass of fish swam as if nothing was lost from the larger fish devouring some of them. Surviving on instinct, their flawless motions and movements never wavered. It is survival; for the few that were eaten, many lived on to reproduce.

In past years, many books and articles have found their way into my vision. I searched for knowledge, understanding, and greater insight into myself and my relationship with the world. Three women in my immediate family were great observers and displayed common sense based on insight and wisdom about human behavior.

My mother often said, "Did you ever notice why people do this?"

I silently stood in front of the aquarium glass and observed the fish communicating in energy of thought transference from one fish to all other fish. They never questioned why they existed. They were just living in the "is-ness," the present, the now.

Why? The never-ending questions in my life did not end with my toddler stage. Parenthood was a new experience—combined with traditions from previous eras. This is the time to nurture another soul in the routine that was established in the ebb and flow of my life. Compared to the traditions and past insights, new thoughts about how to parent felt disconcerting. The book of life of a fish is to live in the is-ness. The presence of nothing more or less - it just is. The book has changed to no longer using the skills of instinct or relying upon past learning experiences from elders.

I sought answers in a famous child-rearing book, but the questions and directions provided no answers. Years later, I found the book was written as a farce—and the author laughed all the way to the bank. He openly stated this on television in an interview. He admitted he never put his children in time-out. He just needed a new age/old thought to write and make money. He did not care if it worked because he did not believe in it. I felt gullible—or did I? The masses of people made the book popular. Why? Why would we turn over our natural instincts to a stranger with no personal concern for the children we gave birth to? It was an observation and a lesson learned. It is similar to the spiritual workshops people attend over and over. Insecurity? The answers are already within them. Their power is there to be owned.

The masses of people sought the safety in numbers like the fish. Books, through the years, have kept the masses swimming in mindless directions. There is an apparent feeling of safety by movement in numbers until the masses no longer question and the misdirected becomes the norm. I sometimes find myself making choices based on instinct and past learning. Seeking the thought process of pondering why and how this is true, in what way does common sense apply to it? What is the basis of my conclusion?

The books are in abundance, in masses like the fish, and it is called the "new wave of spirituality." Is this the natural process of life? Is this so? The band is playing and everyone who seeks safety is marching. Does one have the courage to ask why? To follow the masses is called the norm. Is it okay to be one with the all and retain individuality and personality? Is it a compliment to be called weird? Is it okay not to be one of the group—a fish among fishes? Is it okay to be a person who marches to a different beat than the one the band is playing? Should we play it safe and swim like the fish?

While I was growing up, my grandmother always said, "If someone jumps off the bridge, do you have to? What if you can't swim?" She wholeheartedly promoted common sense and thinking before acting.

Books gave new insights to old thoughts. Thoughts gave stability and safety with their numbers. Thoughts constantly and endlessly ebbed and flowed through my mind. Conscious thought of each individual reaches another mind by thought transference. To swim left and swim right is the motto of a great fish. It is great to be a fish. Do current writers have a better way? Are they repeating what we already know? There are writers who look for profit. Are they taking the proverbial bite into the illusion—or is the mass of fish becoming one big fish. Life is the never-ending drum that beats for all to march in step, or is it?

Does one ask if this is absolutely true? How do I feel about this? Am I going to make my choice or follow the swimming masses ? Am I part of the ocean—or am I the ocean? Am I both? Is there really comfort in being mindless and limitless in the bombardment of another's concept? Can I think for myself and make informed decisions?

By existing in the illusion of now—the is-ness with no past or future—is the only choice to ask why, how, who, where, or when? Is bringing the past and the future into the now making a choice to create change in the moment? Does it create a change in the All? To bring positive change to the school of fish, do we have to embrace life with compassion and being in the is-ness? Life is the All or is it? Being in the flow does not mean getting lost in the flow of life or living like a fish in a fishbowl. Choice is a constant companion.

"Filling the shoes of one adored.
Long ears, a bow tie to boot.
Filling the shoes of one adored.
I am learning how to scoot.
I am living in a new home.
Would someone give me a bone?
I am living in a new home.
I am happy to stay in this home."
—Molly, Jack Russell terrier

Chapter 10

Not Today

Procrastination is a lovely word for not doing what must be done. Will I put off what I am expected to do for myself or others in minutes, days, or longer? "I will … in just a little while." Silently, our internal conversations discuss and rationalize the inevitable procrastination. If we felt that way all the time, what would get done or accomplished? What would never come into existence? Thoughts create inspiration, anxiety creates action, and procrastination creates nothing.

Is it wonderful that procrastination exists? Tomorrow never comes; it is only a dream away. In the daydreaming, I am able to recreate myself. I create what surrounds me with a blink of an eye. It looks like I have done a good job since everything is beautiful or messy to the eye. It will be this way tomorrow, and I can do it tomorrow or the next day. Thank goodness man created time, and I have all of eternity to dream away all the expectations I have created for myself. My mother said, "The dishes will be there tomorrow. Go play with your baby today."

If I continue to ignore the world that calls and beckons me, I can remove myself from this moment of bliss of doing absolutely nothing. "Excuse me a moment … just a little bit longer."

Time to Dream

Dream away during the day, at night, or anytime. A dream of fantasy takes flight under the sun or moon. A dream of fantasy is life in a chair or a bed. Find a place to rest, sit with a throw over my knees, or tuck myself under a blanket in bed. I must get up and get going. There are things to do and places to go. Maybe later—tomorrow or next week, I tell myself. I will just sleep a little bit longer. I must procrastinate the procrastination.

"I praise the light that fulfills my dreams,
I am the universe spinning a song.
I fill my lungs with the winds of time,
I fill my nose with the smell of earth.
I drum the beat of hearts becoming one,
I know the spirit of my soul.
I sing to the sound of whispers becoming one."
—Taos McCloud, Siberian husky

Chapter 11

Happy Hugs

Ouch! Are hugs as delightful as society makes them out to be? Hugs come in a variety of forms: the little squeeze, the cheek-to-cheek hug, a full-length body embrace, the seductive hug, and the proverbial teddy bear hug.

I was not familiar with being hugged constantly—and definitely not by strangers. To enter another's private space, depending on the geographic area one grew up in, can be eighteen inches or more from another person. Entering closer in this cultural space is felt as a threat.

I grew up knowing I was loved without being inundated with hugs. I had three mothers: my biological mother (Bettyann), my mother's mother (Olive), and my mother's sister (Arline). This gave me a preview of what I would look like when I was their age. My great-grandmother (Hannah) had brown hair until she died. None of my three mothers had a gray hair as they aged. Please, God, may I have the same gene? Aunt Arline's neighbor could not tell the four of us apart. She constantly called us by each other's names.

The four of us were a sisterhood. We completed each other's sentences, and we loved Saturday shopping and celebrating personal events in our lives. As the first grandchild—and a girl—they doted on me, but they held back from spoiling me. I thought being the first grandchild was a place of honor until I realized I might die first because of my age!

My grandmother held me while she rocked in that old wicker porch rocker. The seat was large enough to cradle both of us in utmost contentment. As I grew up, I became too big and heavy to be held by grandma in her rocker. It was a devastating loss. The rocking was replaced with sitting next to her on the sofa. As I sat there, she would twirl the curls on the back of my head. My aunt would drive half an hour from work to stroke my face and put me into a restful sleep. When my eyes closed to dream, I felt security. Hugs have many forms.

These three women were ahead of their time. My grandma believed a woman had the right to climb a telephone pole to fix it just like a man. She believed in equality and the same rights for everyone. I was encouraged to become educated because one never knows when a woman will need to support herself or her children. These women had a formidable insight to the world in an era when a woman became old maids at eighteen. Barefoot and pregnant was society's theme. Boys were educated, and girls were not.

I loved and appreciated these wise women's life experiences. They encouraged me to become educated and independent. They said, "Know what you want to do in life, prepare for it, and do it right the first time." I was told not to follow the crowd. It was okay to be different, know who you are, and not assimilate into a crowd.

Their philosophy of life and child-rearing grounded me in ways I had not dreamed. They knew what was what and how to do it. If they did not know something, they admitted it and sought the answer from a reliable source. "Learn something every day—even if it is only one thing" was their motto.

As I watched them raise my three younger brothers and cousins, they always provided support, guidance, and direction to tell the truth. There would be no punishment for what you did if you told the truth.

Back then, people didn't talk about everything as they do now. My grandmother relayed her story of when she asked her mother why the lady had a big belly (pregnant). The response was a slap across the face and a warning not to talk about it. She was told to keep her mouth shut.

In nursing education, I became aware of how these wise women's child-rearing beliefs and practices coincided with pediatric teaching. I would quietly and proudly proclaim pride in them with a simple closed smile. How wise the women in my family were. They searched for the common-sense approach before saying anything or taking action. Gentle talk with direct eye contact results in quiet, interactive children. Gentle, loving touches create balance and well-being. Waiting a little longer before responding allows them to learn to quiet themselves to stay in balance, promoting self-esteem and self-worth. Timely response to an infant's cry provides security and trust. Being held during feedings gave nourishment, emotional support, and love.

I do not remember doctors giving their patients hugs. In later years, doctors encouraged the use of their first names. Being called by your first name reduced the number of lawsuits. People would initiate a lawsuit against Dr. Soandso but not against Harry.

A doctor asked me why an elderly male patient responded to me but would not talk to him even when the exchange was on a first-name basis. I asked the doctor if he shook the patient's hand when he entered the room. He said he did not. In his patient's earlier years, a firm handshake was a man-to-man symbol that showed respect for the other. A handshake was a contract, and the contract was legally binding. A man kept his word, and his handshake was his honor. Many deals were closed with only a handshake. A handshake represented respect. Hugs or handshakes are given out of respect.

The doctor went into the man's room the next morning for rounds and shook the gentleman's hand with his hello. I heard them talking every morning for the remainder of the patient's stay. A handshake opened the door to a doctor-patient relationship, and both men met the needs of the other.

Touch is acknowledgment and provides another means of connection with another living soul. Extending your hand to greet another is respectful and is often met with a response and a smile. Hugs are the same; it is respectful to ask first.

Touch can be appropriate or not. Touching a shoulder or upper arm or hand is okay. Touching reduces blood pressure, lowers heart rates, and produces the endocrine effect. Touch is a nonverbal calming that you are there with them and all is okay.

Later in my life, touch—as designated by the law—could result in sexual harassment if one felt invaded or uncomfortable. In today's society, it is best to ask permission before touching an area to provide medical care. This is best in all situations—medical or not.

The most bonded feeling was when a friend gave me a hug when she met or left me. Occasionally we run into someone whose hug gives noninvasive love. Even blindfolded, I would recognize Mary's beautiful hug. I called her "My Mary." Mary spent her last Christmas evening sharing our friendship in my home. Early on Christmas morning, Mary died of a heart attack.

Months later, I invited Mary's closest friend for lunch. I asked Mary to join us in spirit and give me a sign she was with us. I expected an inanimate object to move or catch a glimpse of her spirit to indicate her presence.

When Fleda arrived, we sat at the dining room table. We were so busy talking, laughing, and eating that I forgot about my request to Mary. All of a sudden, I felt arms around me—giving me the most amazing hug. It was my Mary's hug. It was my first experience with knowing that someone can reach across the veil in spirit to give a physical hug. To this day, when I think of Mary, I remember the feeling of her hugs—and my day becomes brighter.

I awakened in my spirituality to discover there was a need to be with other like-minded people, sharing our inner knowledge and experiences. I had not expected that people equated spirituality with hugs. Hugs without permission from strangers?

Are all hugs benign? No, no, no! While dancing with a man, he would jerk his fist into my spine. It was extremely painful. Men will give a gentle squeeze of a hug in the small of your back to guide the dance. This man would not stop and became upset when I would no longer dance with him. I do not know if his testosterone or insecurity played into this assault. Did he believe this was a hug? Dancing is meant to be a safe and fun experience. Feeling invaded and in pain takes that all away.

I went through an episode of severe pain in my neck, shoulder, and right arm. I could not raise my arms to comb my hair, touch my face, or brush my teeth. Life was painful beyond words. In a store, I could not move my head up or down to see what was on the shelves. My head would not turn, so I refrained from driving. My neck would not support the weight of my head.

Inside my head, I heard my cervical spine cracking. Riding in a car was intolerable—not to mention those Pennsylvania potholes.

The soft tissue between my cervical discs was narrowing and less cushioned. I was informed I would remain in traction for the rest of my life, but I was adamant and stubborn. To this day, I am up walking and going about life.

During that painful time, people would grab me for a hug. A hug pulled my shoulders inward, my neck backward, and my head upward. One hug meant three days of increased pain and decreased mobility. I did not wear a cervical collar, and I was not allowed to. The collar would have indicated to others to not hug me spontaneously. Tactfully, I would ask people not to hug me. I'd say, "Please take my hands." I made sure I extended my hands and offered them in kindness. They would say, "Oh, I know you told me not to hug you, but I just have to." My shoulders would slump, and my body would stiffen at their approach.

Many years of nursing resulted in arthritis between my ribs. I am petite and lifted patients who were much heavier and taller than me. The pain is not frequent, but when it is there, I just want it to stop because it hurts so much. A gentle hug is more than I can bear. When I tactfully ask not to be hugged and offer my hands, people respond as if they had been blatantly insulted. Others say, "I want to hug you anyway." A hug without my permission is a personal invasion of me.

There is another reason I became uncomfortable with people giving me hugs. Some people give hugs to others because they literally have little or no touching or sex in their lives. In nursing education, the example was a widowed grandpa asking a child to sit on his lap. He missed being touched. The intention, most likely, was not to sexual or physical abuse, yet the reason behind the action remains the same, therefore, is an inappropriate means of being touched.

I met a person who felt entitled and became hysterical if I did not allow a hug. Was there was something wrong with me because I would not comply? After all, what is wrong with a hug?

I understand the need for touch and human closeness. People have their own concepts of what is appropriate, and mine is a simple no to being hugged or being told they love me for whatever reason (by strangers). Telling others that you love them frequently is a cult technique to gain control of another person and is called *love bombing*. Are hugs harmless? Yes or no, the answer is within each of us.

Hugs for spouses, children, and family pets are always wonderful and necessary. All others are at the discretion of oneself. I know a new mother with five other children who could not tolerate anyone touching her baby—much less letting another person hold the child—for an entire year. There are animals that indicate by their behaviors that they do not want to be touched. Sentient beings have the right to choose who touches them.

I remember a stranger who stood over me as I sat on a chair and insisted on hugging me. I politely said, "No." I explained that my cervical spine was compressed—and a hug would cause pain. The next thing I knew, I was being powerfully held as I sat on my chair. The hug was so forceful that I lost my breath. The hug was hurting me, and I could not breathe. My chin was over this person's shoulder, and my head was tilted back so far I could not move my mouth to speak. I thought my neck would snap. When I was released, I slumped into the chair. I was in severe pain and felt drained of energy. If the hug had been longer, he would have killed me. My neck would have snapped or my ribs would have broken and punctured my lungs.

The stranger said nothing and walked away. There was no compassion. A hug when used to extract energy from another is a *vampire hug*. I wondered if others felt the same way. I felt raped by his invasion of my personal space and body without permission. Something in his behavior made me feel that he was not a safe person to be near.

Years later, another person invaded my privacy and insisted on a hug. The ultimate goal was to do a psychic invasion. I psychically blocked this person from retrieving any information. One does not have to touch another to know who a person is. An adequate psychic would never have to insist on a hug to know another.

Are hugs benign or malevolent? How does the hug make you feel? Were you imposed upon? Was the meaning of the hug overt or covert? Did you feel your energy force being drained? Did you wish the hug would end? It is always a choice to be the recipient of a hug. Respect others by asking—and comply with the answer.

Loving hugs are intended for sharing joy, respect of family, and friendship. Embrace those in need of comfort. In the wondrous moments of life, hold, hug, rock, or snuggle your children in your arms in pure love and contentment. Lovingly hug the animals you have welcomed into your family; they are there to love you unconditionally.

A hug may be a soft whisper that thanks you for being you. There are many reasons for giving or receiving hugs. They are the physical connections of souls. Embraces encompass each other and create sacred circles. Hugs should leave one feeling loved, safe, or comforted. Share a very gentle cheek hug and notice how a respectful hug brings a smile.

"Dance with me,
All through life, all through strife.
Dance with me,
All through joy, all through sad.
Dance with me,
All through smiles, all through tears.
Dance with me,
All through health, all through ills.
Dance with me,
All through days, all through nights.
Dance with me,
All through hope, all through dreams.
Dance with me,
All through faith, all through love."
—Sugar Plum Faerie, a domestic mouse

Chapter 12

Quilt

Piece it together with thread and needle, stitch by stitch. Life is a patchwork quilt. It may be designed from cut fabric or a patch of scraps put together at random. Sometimes a quilt is thought out, and sometimes it is spontaneous in its journey. Stitching a quilt does not go awry. The best plans may fit together like a puzzle only to become scrambled by some unseen incident. Would we prefer life to be perfect in its progression with our hopes, dreams, and expectations? Would we prefer life to be an experience of the unforetold?

The spontaneous journey brings all factors of childhood, youth, adulthood, and the end stages of life to bring forth its wisdom from experience. Our minds decipher the problems and the alternative solutions to a comfortable outcome.

Is there perfection? Yes, we see it in nature, the universe, and the infant in our arms. The rose holds a beauty that is indescribable—or is it described with individual perception? Innocent perception is an accurate recollection of what is observed, and the entirety of the observation is accurately recalled in the mind.

Would perfection have a place or be boring? Some nuns knit to sell their products to create funds to help others. Each garment has one deliberately placed flaw in it because the only perfection is God.

God sees us as perfection. He created us. Perfection comes from non-judgment. I look at a quilt and envision the person who created it. The quilt speaks of the individuality and the personal choice to create. Life is like stitching a quilt. What does yours look like?

"Day and night, I am one,
Daylight, I am the sun.
Nightlight, I am the moon,
Ever changing from sun to moon.
From moon to sun, this is fun,
My light shines, I am One."
—Candy, Siberian husky

Chapter 13

Friggatriskaidekaphobia

What a long word—twenty-three letters. It is a fear of Friday the Thirteenth. In 2011, Friday the Thirteenth was the only Friggatriskaidekaphobia for the entire year.

There are many thoughts relating to bad luck or superstition for this marked day. The long word comes from the Norse goddess and the fear of the number thirteen. Judas was the thirteenth person at the Last Supper. The thirteenth floor of a high-rise is labeled the fourteenth floor due to superstition. The list of coincidences for the number thirteen is prevalent.

A friend celebrated his birthday on Friday the Thirteenth. It did not appear to him that it was a negative time. To him, it meant good luck since it was his birthday. The day was always a positive and happy one for him.

The things we incorporate from history or unfounded beliefs are deeply ingrained into our subconscious minds. It is bad luck to walk under a ladder, open an umbrella indoors, or have a sparrow enter the house (means death). There are many sayings and major events in our lives that cling to our superstitious natures. Even so, we hold on to them and make them real to ourselves. Many serial killers have names that total thirteen letters; maybe there is more than meets the eye.

As the saying goes, be careful what you wish for because it may come true. It is a fair warning to not say aloud or think what is negative. What we put into the universe is what the universe gives us in return. What goes round comes around is known as karma. Each day is a monitoring of what we think or say, and the universe is listening.

Humans like to frighten themselves with scary movies, scaring others, violent games, and more. Why do we do this? Is it pent-up energy to be released or based in our fears or our coliseum nature. The human desire for the gory aspect of shock or horror in witnessing the torture or demise of another human or animal?

How do we diminish the negative thoughts that ramble incessantly in our minds? The chatter never seems to stop. It gets louder when we try to make it go away. Mind chatter can be diminished or released. An easy, uneventful way is to hold your head, look forward, look up at the ceiling without moving your head, and then bring your eyes back to the position of looking forward. The chatter will stop temporarily and make you feel peaceful. These few moments of silence are rejuvenating. The mind chatter likes to keep us hopping. Eventually, the chatter will bug us again.

We change the world by being that change within us. Superstition can be fun if kept to a minimum without the intent of escalating into violence. It helps to leave the horror movie and scary television shows to others. Though fictional, the computer images are very lifelike. To the literal child, if it looks real, it must be true.

Seeking the meaning of a superstition may appear ridiculous. The meaning you give Friday the Thirteenth is what you make it. Make it a joyful one. The calendar holds another Friday we celebrate called Good Friday. Good luck, good fortune—and start Friday the Thirteenth by making a good wish.

Karen Kober

The Way

Candlelight, angel bright,
Guide us to his light.
Starlight, moon bright,
Shine on us this night.
Love, joy, peace, miracle,
Celebration, goodwill,
From stars to earth,
From life to death,
From light to dark,
From smiles to tears.
Journey the long road,
One breath at a time,
One heartbeat at a time,
Words to make rhyme.
Our spirits guide the way,
Our souls step the way,
The candle lights the way,
The starlight shines the way.
We are not alone.

Chapter 14

How's the Weather?

"People who talk in the context of the weather are difficult for you. You need productive conversation to feel comfortable."

This is me. Talking about the weather is okay and makes me feel secure. It is difficult to remember how often the weather was talked about in one small conversation. I found it astounding that sometimes nothing other than the weather was discussed. Concepts challenge those who only want to feel safe. Is this negative? No, it is just a need to feel secure

Productive conversation may imply a hope or bring an a-ha moment to inspire someone else to incorporate an awareness or concept. It may bring about change in knowing who one is or create positive changes. We nourish ourselves with new perspectives.

A defense mechanism is to remain closed to new thoughts, concepts, and current trends in the workforce or society. A person who uses defense mechanisms has a need to feel safe and in the status quo. It is their issue alone. Just accept them with grace. A defense mechanism provides a safe feeling, yet it is detrimental to mental or emotional health when it impacts daily living.

Life is fun and joyful when it is prevalent in our lives. An open mind holds promise to gain insight to our world (seen and unseen). An open mind opens the heart. The weather changes, and life changes our insights and wisdom to grow from within.

Change is constantly present in movement (inward and outward). I hear people say they wish the sun would shine every day without any other weather changes. My inner instinct says this is boring and dangerous; without change, nothing grows. The rain is needed for watering the earth. Lightning provides nitrogen for plant growth. The wind carries seeds from one place to another. The sun's rays provide energy for production of chlorophyll and nutrients for growth for living creatures and plants. In life's harmony, all cycles of life are dependent on everything in existence. A break in the cycles creates unbalance, disaster, and disease.

Change within us and around us creates change for growth. How boring life would be if we were only allowed to color in the coloring books that were given to us as children—constantly instructed to color within the lines. In third grade, I was given a large sheet of paper to color and crayons to draw something about Thanksgiving. It was an opportunity to color what I thought it represented.

Bored or tired of coloring and feeling restricted, I dashed different bright colors on the trees for autumn leaves. My teacher said she wanted to put my picture on the bulletin board until I ruined it with the dashes of color. I refused to be confined or change the drawing. I left it as I created it. I did not care if it was on the bulletin board or not. That was not the point. The drawing was mine. Change and creativity are inevitable within each of us and will explode into personal expressions of who we are. We are the artists of our lives.

Ritual is a way of feeling secure and safe. Everyone needs rituals. Try putting on the opposite shoe than you usually do first thing in the morning. Check to see if you feel uneasy throughout the day. Rituals are important. Defense mechanisms are how we subconsciously protect ourselves from outside influences. They are not mentally or emotionally healthy when they hinder our daily lives.

Life is about change in all aspects. From conception to death, we experience progressive and irreversible changes. Life changes us. Life changes the world as we know it. Gone are the heavy black telephones with operators who connect us to another person by three digits. Credit card-sized phones give us the freedom to talk with many people at the same time all around the world. Even these will change with continued research and the drive for something better to increase sales.

Life is interesting if we allow positive change and responsibilities to envelop our lives. We are responsible for our continued existence on this earth. God gave us the earth and our vows to love and protect it. It is a marriage to the earth, which we call home. If we actively nurture and protect the earth, we leave a healthy place for our great-grandchildren's great-grandchildren and so forth. It would be devastating to witness the death of our families, humanity, and earth if we did not treat this beautiful planet as a marriage to love, honor, and protect.

At times, I become weary of the spiritual mindlessness I witness. There are four stages or aspects to spiritual growth. The first, an individual is unaware or often referred to as asleep. A pattern of living by what others believed to be true and instilled into their perception. The second is awakening or referred to as blossoming like a rose. This individual feels uneasy with the pattern of only knowing what others have told them. They are starting to question if there is something more to life and themselves. They start seeking answers to why they are here, what is their purpose. The third individual has awakened to the awareness God exists and is in everything including themselves. The fourth is chosen by God for a certain task. In commitment to God they receive the Nine Gifts of Discernment. It includes becoming psychic, a healer, protected and provide for by God, speak and hear in tongue. They have an inner knowing of truth, wisdom and guidance from God, spirit guides and angels. This is a journey from the safety net of being told what to think or believe, individual curiosity and questions, and acceptance of truth. They seek themselves inwardly honoring the God within them.

What spiritual evolvement does another person present to you in conversation? Is everything as it is? Are we mindful of the changes happening in our marriage to the earth and its life forms? Is it apathetic to elude the responsibility to nurture and protect the earth by letting the other guy do it? We are the other guy. The objection to learn pertinent information requires self-action to maintain a healthy world, and self is what holds truth.

Will we become a headline in the afternoon media reports? Does it always happen to the other guy? The destruction of our earth only involves the other guys. Will the government take care of the earth? or us? We say, "Let some organization or somebody else do it."

The world we live in is only an illusion—or so proclaim its ardent spiritual students. We do not need to intervene because it is not real. Are we not part of the illusion? When we are present, we are part of the illusion of choice. When something happens between two people, we rationalize that it is their illusion or their script. When we are present and become part of the script, it is no longer another illusion—it is ours. We are the web of life, and we are connected with all life and the earth. Earth is our family and our home. What one person does impacts the balance of creation with a positive or negative outcome.

There is hope. The Solar Logo, mass pyramiding of the Christ consciousness, will positively change our concept and living patterns to bring harmony and mindfulness. The Solar Logo and the Second Coming started in the summer of 2011. In this beginning of the thousand years of peace, the joyful experience of life prevails in Yeshua's words when he speaks of us living in joy. Love is a misused word. "One brings joy when one brings, radiates, and expresses joy. When one brings joy, one gives love." In our mindfulness, we will create and enjoy the true blessings of life. We are given life to learn, grow, and to take care of our earth and creation. It is a gift from God.

"Dashing here, dashing there,
Most everywhere,
I am smart and fast.
Winning titles, winning games,
Is my middle name,
I am smart and fast.
Looking here, looking there,
Looking everywhere,
I am smart and fast.
Winning here, winning there,
Winning everywhere,
I am smart and fast."
—Magic, Jack Russell terrier

Chapter 15

Irritant

It itches! It stings! It cramps! Are the simple irritants in life the real irritants in life?

People who actively practice spirituality find it difficult to cope with the irritants from other people. People who are disrespectful, insincere, angry, abusive, unkind, aggressive, insulting, and obnoxious make demeaning comments to other people. What do we do with this constant unprovoked bombardment? Is it a kind and gentle person's proclamation?

We have experienced these verbal, nonverbal, and physical assaults. We walk away perplexed and are often too confused to figure it out. How are we going to respond? Our minds try to push it down into our hearts. It is easy to lovingly say these people are God's children and their behavior is a cry for love, but we feel dumbfounded and perplexed.

We have a small eight-pound Yorkie named Elf. In a store, he suddenly and unexpectedly barked vigorously at a man who walked past us. I did not catch what had happened until the man—in a business suit—turned and walked past us again. He hissed at Elf. My thoughts rambled. Was it a random event? What was the origin of this behavior? Does he abuse animals, children, or adults in his personal life? Does he interact negatively in business?

I took a deep breath, checked my inner feelings, delayed my response, and remained silent. What he thought he was doing to Elf—or me—he was only doing to himself. It was his issue. I silently blessed him and walked away. I thanked Elf for his protective warning about the negative man near me.

An immediate response on my part might have escalated it into a violent situation. Now is the moment to make another choice in the immediate situation. Should I have chosen the outward display of kindness, compassion, and forgiving? At times, it is done silently. Holding one's own power is most effective when walking away. Holding power is important, especially for women in our male-dominated society. Women tend to give away their power. Women are paid less than men, are ruled over for promotions, and are abused in some relationships.

Is it rude to walk away? No! One does not allow negative behaviors to gain an audience. Negative behaviors stop when there is no secondary gain derived from those the assault is directed to. If the behavior continues without an audience, there is an underlying psyche/social problem. Walking away indicates that one is in charge and is demanding respect. We do not want to give the energy a place to grow out of control. Bless and release the emotion and the person to neutralize the situation.

This behavior was a cry for love. Something was missing in his life. All behavior has a point of origin. We can change our behaviors with family or friends and observe the outcomes. With strangers, there is no verbal context in the situation. Realizing every person is doing the best they can in any given moment shows compassion. Yeshua says there will always be those people in the world. We should ignore them and be with those who are walking in the kindness of humanity.

What else may be learned from our encounter with this man? Patience is the most difficult emotion to hold onto. We are a fast-food, microwave society. We want it now—if not yesterday. Patience can be very trying—whether it is a mosquito buzzing in your ear or a person being obnoxious. Patience is not allowing another to disrespect the God within you.

We live our lives as witnesses to abuse, especially with defenseless children and animals. We are present for a reason and should intervene for the helpless. The world is changing into a world of peace and kindness. It is coming, and with patience, it will arrive soon. Pray for those who are negatively impacting society; they are having a difficult time. They are the farthest from God. There is hope. Truly, there is hope.

"Jump for joy, leap with passion,
Stir giggles round and round.
Hop into hearts, skip with laughter,
Blow bubbles into heaven.
Life is happy, gleeful, giddy,
Chuckles, and delightful screams."
—Snickers, beagle

Chapter 16

Joyful Sun

Peeking through the trees was the first glimpse of the soft, wispy yellow of the dawning sun in the eastern horizon. It streamed its soft light upon the morning dew. The dew in its reflections mirrored the surrounding life in each drop. The reflective sparkles shine for all to witness the beauty provided by the sun. When our internal awareness leads us to focus on the uniqueness of life, it is a spiritual intervention. There is something special for us to become aware of and something for us to learn. A personal message is given to move us forward on our spiritual journeys.

We encounter the creation of God opening our hearts and souls and entering a deep cleansing calmness. The misty morning is the breath of God, and we inhale the fragrance of the moist earth in its beginning of a new dawn. Flowers unfold and raise their heads from the darkness of the night to the eternal radiance of sunshine. The warmth of a joyful sun embraces our spirits in the rebirth of each moment.

A day in the sun's rays entices many a heart into exuberance from playing, dancing, swimming, skiing, skating, camping, picnicking, and enjoying other fun outdoor activities. The sun's golden glow shines upon us, and nature gives us nourishment to grow and live. Soil is pushed away by a tiny new plant in its effort to reach life in the sun. The sunrays stream through the trees and light the plants beneath them. Nothing else in life can give a sparkling dance on the rippling water of lakes, rivers, streams, and ponds. The warm beach sand gives us many hours to create sculptures from the sands of time. We relax every muscle in our bodies when we bury our toes deep into the sun-drenched sand.

There are more stars in the universe than there are grains of sand on the entire earth. We try to perceive the scope and vastness of our universe beyond our limited comprehension. It is a blessing to feel minute in comparison to the galaxies—too many to count and so many not witnessed. Galaxies create suns. A sun is a star. In our miniscule world, we are aware that we are not even the size of a microbe in the existence beyond our world, yet we are here in the blessed miracle called life.

We are covered and filled with microbes, parasites, and flora. Some are destructive, and others we cannot live without. We are a world unto them. These communities are not forefront in our consciousness. We look outward as if the world begins and ends with us.

There are souls that venture out into our universe and seek something different and unknown. Here, I feel safe and comfortable to experience the sun, moon, stars, wind, and rain. Life is a window; turn away for a few moments. Look again and notice the changes from the moment before. We are unable to recapture each day and make the sun shine upon us again. Our view of the earth changes throughout the day as the world spins its way around the sun.

It is refreshing to have a picnic in the morning sun. The air smells sweet and fresh. The morning moisture cleans the air, and everything feels cool and damp. The breakfast on the grill makes us hungry. The coffeepot perks rapidly and fills our nostrils with an aroma not to be missed. A quiet interlude is heard between the doves singing their sunrise songs.

At sunrise or sunset, we can look directly at the red sun and feel empowered to receive undiscovered nutrients. The sunrise turns from pink to yellow on a bright day. The morning feels warmer and warmer as the sun soars up into the sky. Grab a plate, a fork, and a cup of coffee; the best is yet to come as we sit under the dawning sun.

Time

What do I say? Where do I go?
Do I say nay? Do I lie low?
Now is the time; pray for the soul.
Is life complex? Is life psychosis?
Is life simple? Is life neurosis?
Now is the time; pray for the soul.
What do I say? Where do I go?
Do I say nay? Do I lie low?
Now is the time; pray for the soul.
Is life sunny, under the sun?
Is life funny, under the sun?
Now is the time; pray for the soul.
What do I say? Where do I go?
Do I say nay? Do I lie low?
Now is the time; pray for the soul.
Is life boring? Is life grilling?
Is life rousing? Is life thrilling?
Now is the time; pray for the soul.
What do I say? Where do I go?
Do I say nay? Do I lie low?
Now is the time; pray for the soul.

Chapter 17

Keyboard Kitty

The house felt warm and cozy as I pressed my nose against the window and peered out at the star-filled winter night. The beauty of the silent snowfall was broken by the sound of the phone ringing. My friend's voice filled the earphone with scrambled words and tears. Mark, her green-eyed white cat, was in the hospital.

My friend, Janice, was driving home from her job as a nurse. The headlights showed Mark unmoving on the road by her home. How she spotted a white cat in the white snow was a miracle. She picked him up and rushed him to the veterinarian hospital. Her voice tense with panic, she asked what happened to Mark.

As an animal communicator, nurse, and friend, my heart dropped. I connected quickly with Mark since I had been the voice for Mark before. Mark said he was hit by a car. With his last bit of strength, he mustered himself onto the road, knowing that she would find him. He did not want to die without her holding him. Mark sent the message of being in unbearable pain, and the physical damage to his organs was beyond survival. He asked her to release him into spirit. He wanted out of the intolerable pain.

Animals have taught me that their concept of death is different from humans. They know they will return from the physical body into spirit again and again. It is the philosophy of the animal kingdom.

Janice understood Mark's plea for help and asked the vet to euthanize him. The vet responded with his belief in Mark's survival. I talked with Mark after the vet refused to euthanize him. Mark begged for help going home. He was too weak to cross over, and his pain was beyond what he could bear. He pleaded and pleaded for help with being released from his body.

I told Janice that Foxx and I would help Mark in two ways. First, we would send Mark healing energy to ease his pain. Energy healing is sending loving energy for comfort or healing. It would help Mark cross over if that was for his highest good. The energy can be sent a long distance and is very powerful. The energy comes from God, and the practitioner is the vehicle through which he sends his loving healing. Second, we would send loving energy to the vet so he could become aware of Mark's needs and open his heart for Mark's request.

The vet held his conviction that Mark would survive. He refused to euthanize Mark for two more days. From nursing, I know some physicians have difficulty accepting death. I was not sure if this was the vet's issue or his true belief that Mark would make it. Animals have shorter life spans and are here to teach us about death. We do not die. Animals accept physical and etheric life as one eternal life.

Mark was declining rapidly, and the vet finally conceded that Mark was not going to survive because his injuries were too severe.

Euthanasia was planned as soon as she could get there to share her last moments with Mark and say good-bye to him. I was aware of the time for injection when I witnessed Foxx's physical body next to the rocking chair. His front paws were stretched out in front of him. He had his head flat on the floor between his front legs. He reverently closed his eyes and appeared in a trance.

I sent transitioning energy to Mark. In my holy eye was the beautiful moment where one's own heart fills with love and skips a beat. Foxx had white fur and blue eyes, and Mark had white fur and green eyes; they moved up and to the right, disappearing into a cloud of nothingness.

Foxx slowly opened his eyes, wobbled to his feet, and stumbled out to the hallway. The expenditure of energy had left him woozy. Just as quickly, he came bouncing back into the family room as his usual self. He honored me by allowing me to witness how he physically and spiritually experienced helping another cross over into heaven. My heart swelled with gratitude and pride; Foxx is the prayer in my heartbeat. He allowed me to witness the spiritual love he gave to Mark by crossing him into heaven.

Foxx said Mark's message to his human guardian was that he crossed over easily. He was out of pain and felt so good after the long, tortuous ordeal. He wanted her to know he loved her so much that he would be coming back to live with her again. Mark, knowing his guardian liked white cats, mentioned he already planned to return to her as a differently colored cat.

My friend was sobbing in grief and found comfort in Mark's message. She would really have liked him to come back as a white cat because of her love for white cats. She paused and said she would love him in any color. She would be grateful just to hold him in her arms again. I finished my conversation and told her not to look for Mark. Mark would create a universal opportunity to get back to her. She would know him immediately because of a strong bonding feeling or a familiar behavior.

A few months later Janice called. There were no tears this time— only total excitement. She had stopped by the vet's office and seen a tiger-colored kitten. I could sense her yearning to put this little one in her arms. It was Mark I assured her. She kept saying, "I knew it. I knew it." I could sense the biggest grin on her face, and I could hear it in her voice.

My friend named the kitten Juliette. While talking with Janice, Juliette asked for a second name. Her second name became Jean. Juliette Jean was elated about her new name. It was just what she wanted.

Juliette Jean has enveloped her guardian's heart with purring love—and her computer keyboard with her paws. My friend says she has a problem sending e-mails because Juliette Jean is always there to help her type.

"Blessed is our creation that speaks his name,
Blessed is our devotion that calls his name,
Blessed is our compassion that loves his name.
Blessed is our hope that knows his name,
Blessed is our love that is his name,
Blessed is our heart that feels his name.
Blessed is our desire to share his name,
Blessed is our knowing to give his name,
Blessed is our honor to be his name."
—Mark, cat

Chapter 18

Laxity or Apathy?

Laxity is the state of being slack. Does laxity imply a lack of initiative? Have we, as a society, become lax—or is it apathy? Apathy is a lack of compassion or concern. I asked myself this question upon viewing the tall, heavyset youth strike back after three years of taunting abuse from a smaller boy. It was on video, yet it held a powerful visual impact as if I were there. The youth seemed aware enough of the constant teasing to brush it off and ignore the smaller boy. He gently brushed away the other boy's poking arm. The video was about the breaking point when enough is enough. The proverbial last straw was when the youth slammed the aggressor. The visual tugged at my tummy, and my heart felt like it flipped.

After watching the video, my mind was flooded with questions. Why didn't the parents intervene to limit the behavior or encourage a conversation between the boys? Why hadn't the boys told their parents about the three years of abuse? Did they feel safe enough to tell an adult? Why had the adults who witnessed the episode not intervened before, during, or after the crisis? Why was the educational institution not taking an active role in stopping the bullying behavior?

Bullying is preventable when behavioral expectations of are met and followed through on. The father of the victim claimed that his son had not told him about it. Did the boy not want to be a tattletale? The mother of the bully was defensive about her son's behavior. My first thought was to pray for the mother and her son since they were the farthest from God.

Is bullying new to society? No. It is as old as mankind, and I may not judge it. Has the behavior increased over the past several generations? One may answer yes to this question. I may judge how viewing the video conflicts with my value system. It becomes an observation of behavior that needs to be corrected.

I was raised with no tolerance for verbal, emotional, or physical abuse of any individual or group. My grandpa frequently said, "A man is no longer a man when he hits a woman." I was expected to stand firm against any abuse or degradation against me or anyone else. Respect and courtesy were the key words in the world around me as I grew up. As an adult, the message was no tolerance for others who attacked the God within me or others.

My very young child spoke to me about two other girls pressuring her to verbally hurt another girl. I knew this behavior was called the pecking order, a need to feel superior to another. Our child did not like what the others were doing to the girl and did not want to be part of it. She said she would not like it to be done to her. She was under peer pressure. I told her to apologize to the girl for any hurt she may have caused and to apologize to the teacher for her personal behavior. I was proud of her courage. Her teacher admired her truth and courage. Our child marked this event with self-respect and compassion for another. She felt the inner peace to be free of the situation.

Some people take the attitude that kids will be kids, but it does not apply to negative, harmful situations or outcomes. Does bullying lead to rage and school shootings? Does violence cause apathy toward violence in the news, on television, and in movies? Viewing violence decreases the impact, and when it no longer shocks us, it may lead to apathy.

There was a time when high school teacher posed two questions to her students:

> Was the atomic bombing of another country, which produced many deaths and years of radiation from the land causing cancer, acceptable?

> Response: It was okay as long as the buildings remained unharmed.

71

A few teenagers broke into a department store during the night. Was this the right thing to do?

Response: It was okay to break in as long as they did not steal anything.

It appeared the value of life from the opinions of the students devalued the life of others. It would have been more interesting if there were two more questions:

What if you and your family were living in that country?

What if your home or business was broken into?

It was the first time I heard myself scream. I fell to my knees after slipping on a wet floor. Two men helped me to my feet. Other people around me remained in place. They looked, but they never moved a foot toward me or asked if I was okay. Those who instinctively respond usually have spiritual or medical backgrounds. Those who did not respond perplexed me.

As I watched the bullying video, I wondered if the victim felt the same way? Was this the coliseum effect? In the coliseum effect, there is a human need to view the gore or demise of another being. Was it a safety net? Why do people gawk at backed-up traffic?

In the past, I had a seasonal job where I talked with people on the phone from all over the world. A gentleman from California said it was better that the planes crashed on the East Coast (the World Trade Center) than where he was. After a few days of phone calls, no one talked about the impact of the terrorist event. It was just another media story from the past. Sadness for those lives lost brought greed to sell products. People were profiting from pain, and grief became a collectable to remember. The amount of money spent could have been put to better use. Do I need something in my home to remember that event?

As a registered nurse, I worked in an institution where violence could erupt at any moment. The morning started with two large men getting in a fistfight. I cringed inside and found myself between the men's flying fists. It was horrible to hear fists hitting another's body.

I had never heard that before. Pointing at the chairs, I yelled, "You sit there—and you sit there." They looked down, surprised, and sat down. The confrontation ended.

I was astonished that I had intervened impulsively. The situation could have been deadly. Somewhere inside us, there is a compulsion to help. Where does this strength come from? How does one jump into a river to save another? Does the possibility of two lives lost instead of one make common sense? Somewhere it is in all of us.

The other drivers looked at me like I was nuts when I pulled over to help the accident victims. The traffic filed by, and drivers slowed down for a moment to gawk before continuing on.

How was it acceptable that the adults who knew of the bullying did not stop it for three years? Did they not want to get involved? As adults in a teaching environment, they were involved because they were present. Let the "other guy" take care of it. What if you are the other guy? Adults are responsible for the actions of children. We must guide them and help them grow up as civilized human beings with acceptable behavior.

I've witnessed individuals who did not pass me by when I needed help. The kindness of one person restored my belief in mankind. It reminded me of a Christmas war story. Two men on opposing sides stopped attacking each other. Neither spoke the same language, yet they found themselves in a stranger's home for the holiday meal. There are moments when time stands still allowing even enemies to have a moments of camaraderie to share the reverence of peace.

Old Folk Song

I walked a mile with Pleasure,
She chatted all the way,
Leaving me none the wiser,
With all she had to say.
I walked a mile with Sorrow,
Never a word said she,
But, O, the thing I learned from her,
When Sorrow walked with me.
—Unknown

Chapter 19

McGinty

Telepathic communicators hear in different ways. I hear sentient beings telepathically speak to me as if I am hearing a human voice talk including their accent and expressions. It does not matter where they are or what they are doing. If they speak another language the universe translates it into English.

"McGinty." I heard Elf telepathically talk in a loud and clear voice as he turned and trotted away. "What do you mean?" I asked as he reached the family room door and disappeared around the corner. "Come back here." I yelled to Elf.

Elf returned and said he had lived a past life as a farmer in the late 1700s. He looked strong and had a deep, furrowed brow. The sun had taken its toll over the years. He had shoulder-length gray hair and a matching beard. He wore farm clothes or the attire of a bagpiper. He looked very stunning in his kilts.

Elf, known then as Sean McGinty, lived in County Cork, Ireland. He told me his wife's name was Margaret. They had two lads, John and James, and a lassie named Rose.

Elf said, "All the pipes played." Sean must have had many friends in his life because the bagpipes at his funeral were felt deeply by his spirit as he watched and listened. The bagpipes honored their fallen friend and fellow piper. Elf showed pride in his eyes when he talked about the pipes.

"My Irish dog.", I pondered silently. A "Knocker"—half-leprechaun on his father's side and German fairy on his mother's side—Kelsey was noted for sitting on Elf's shoulders. Knockers lived in the mines of Pennsylvania. They knocked to warn miners of impending disasters. They only requested three things: no signing of the cross, swearing, or whistling. The fae had a different spirituality and were not a religious institution. The signing of the cross is an insult to them.

Kelsey wore his big-brimmed brown hat, a white shirt, a brown vest, brown pants, and knee-high black boots. He rode Elf and had a high old time going where Elf took him. He cared a lot for Elf, but he could be too much for him sometimes. Kelsey had to be reminded to get down from Elf's shoulders and stand beside him.

One morning, I witnessed Elf with his front paws forward and his back legs standing. That position indicated an honorary bow. Kelsey was introducing Elf to his new teacher, Cocoa. Cocoa was a faerie. The bow of honor was for him. Elf would be seen many times in deep discussion with Cocoa.

"Blessed be, nearer to thee,
I sing praises of above.
Blessed be, nearer to thee,
Song, poem, prayer, all are love.
Walk with me, walk with thee,
Step lightly, step with fire.
Walk with me, walk with thee,
The path leads, heart's desire.
Blessed be, nearer to thee,
Love flowers from small seeds.
Blessed be, nearer to thee,
Love powers all my needs."
—Elf McMagic, Yorkshire terrier

Chapter 20

Oak Leaves and Acorns

The green leaves are fading to bring forth their inner beauty and color. The birds are gathering and look like clothespins on the telephone wires. The tall grass is changing its summer hues to golden and rusty colors. The marigolds in autumn deepen and intensify the color of their blooms. The air feels crisper in anticipation of autumn turning into winter, and a cool breeze brushes our cheeks. Autumn is pumpkin pie time with its aroma of cinnamon and nutmeg. The little children with huge backpacks look like turtles as they stand on the corner waiting for the school bus One can hear them laughing, giggling, and chattering as they scramble up the yellow banana steps to be transported to their first day of school.

Life edges forward, and I know that the life within is inseparable from all that exists. We are always changing with the earth in awareness and physically toward the final spectrum of life. We ponder the forward movement of life unseen: thousands of monarch butterflies migrating south, bears feeding to satiation for hibernation and birth of their young, the changing of the fur on the white-tailed deer from a warm summer tan to the darkened camouflage of winter, the V formation of Canada goose in flight, and acorns plopping to earth with tiny thuds. So much happens out of reach of my everyday sight during autumn in nature's preparation for winter.

It tickles my tummy to hear the crunching sound when kicking dry leaves on the sidewalk. It's a carpet of colors: orange, yellow, red, green, and all variation of these colors combined. Traveling along a country road, I notice dried cornstalks, milkweed pods spilling white parachute seeds into the air, and rolled hay. All colors, hues, and textures are represented in decorating our home for autumn. Pumpkins, candles, wheat, leaves, wreaths, Indian corn, harvest fruit, dried oranges, and rose hips fragrance the air while scarecrows hold vigilance in the fields.

The warm colors of autumnal grace speak from the warm calmness inside of me. I gently rock back and forth in my grandmother's wicker rocker and daydream. I watch the leaves swirl down from the trees. The pumpkin-orange afghan I am knitting for a gift is almost finished. The black cast-iron wood stove's fire dances, crackles, sputters, and spurts its orange-red flames. Hot chocolate steams cocoa under my nose mixed with the aromas coming from the oven. The aroma filters through the house of baking pumpkin bread and cranberry-nut bread. Warm sugar cookies cool on racks and wait to be frosted. These baked goodies are to be frozen for the upcoming holiday celebration with family and friends.

Autumn is a time to celebrate the season of harvest and gratitude for its abundance. Every morning throughout the year is exemplified in autumn as the forefront of hope and desire to witness the beauty of autumn and the musty smell of dried leaves that have fallen to the ground. Autumn speaks of our yearning and the realization that we have lived another harvest, grateful for food and life: a cornucopia of joy, love, family, and the people we have met along the way. The autumnal harvest of peace is felt in mellow days. Autumn passes with a lowering sun and a harvest moon.

Pumpkin Polka

Oh, oh the Pumpkin Polka!
By pumpkin's light, black cat frights,
By witch's flight, its Hallow night,
Oh, oh the Pumpkin Polka!
Sneak up and down the long, dark street,
Knock on doors and yell trick or treat,
Candy corn, chocolate delights,
Halloween hopscotch, vampire bites.
Gold leaves fall 'tis a scary night,
Shadows bend in eerie moonlight,
Spider webs, big black bats,
Sinewy smoke, and witch hats.
Bones do rattle, witches cackle,
Not another football tackle,
See-through ghosts bound in shackles,
Scary ghosts cry and hackle.
Skulls and bones cross the path,
Hurry past, run by fast,
Lil' goblins hide in scary masks,
Halloween Polka makes feet dance.
Don't stop and stare, you'll get scared,
Turn three times, if you are dared,
Jump to the left, jump to the right,
Let's do the polka through the night.
Halloween costumes, witches' capes,
Devils' pitchforks, it's getting late,
Bags of goodies, oh my footsies,
Someone please rub my old tootsies!
Let's dance, dance another dance,
Ichabod's horse likes to prance,
Please, please, Ichabod, don't fall,
Apples bob, the polka calls.

Chapter 21

Grace

"Love is what we are here to learn ... love only exists in the presence of honor and respect. Death is what we are here to experience ... death is the transformation of our physical into the spirit. Rebirth is what we are here to relearn ... rebirth is the knowing that we are eternal. Love, death, and rebirth are cycles in the trinity of life. A glimpse into the past is the trace of which we were and a journey in the future is walking the time line. Neither exists—there is only now."

—W.A. Foxx (June 3, 1997–August 9, 2010)

Yesterday no longer exists; it cannot be recreated. Tomorrow is mysterious; it holds uncertainty. Will it be created as we expect or desire? Will God choose each moment for us? Will we experience freedom to allow him to choose each moment? Neither yesterday nor tomorrow exists in the present reality of now.

How do I live in the now? I live each moment as a choice for love and release expectations, judgments, and comparisons. Life was created with purpose to care for our earth and experience spiritual growth. Nothing is greater than another in our accountability to honor and respect the oneness that we, the earth, and the universe remain healthy and balanced. The word comparison is the gentler definition, and observation holds clarity.

How easy it is to put oneself into the trap of what does not exist. A reflection, a dream, or a mystery is a fleeting moment. What exists in life is what is seen, heard, experienced, and felt now. All is as it is now. It is just as easy to accept and experience the now in the fullness of love. By experiencing life in conscious awareness, we are present in each moment of time. Animals only live in the now with unconditional love. Honor and respect are higher. It is like being in heaven without the constraints of time and space since humans created them.

We are here to cherish every moment of life in each moment. This creates contentment to surrender the yesterday and tomorrow of its nonexistent expectation, judgment, comparisons, and living in the moment. In each moment, we live in joy as we journey toward our heavenly home.

"Fly into dreams and wisp away into fantasy,
Tip your outstretched arms to turn about,
Lift your head to fly and roll over to fly down.
Fly as fast as you can, for flight feels free,
Fly to the stars, to the moon and back,
Fly in circles to the left and to the right.
Soar higher than eagles, and glide faster than kites,
Fly past the present and into the future,
Fly into dreamland and wisp away into heaven."
—Kristy, Irish setter

Chapter 22

Insatiable Quest

Insatiable quest leads to several thoughts of knowledge, passion, change, curiosity, growth, learning, desire, and anxiety. It is driven, and it never ends. Our souls become curious and seek answers to the unknown. We endeavor to expand our knowledge. We are challenged in new ways to understand the world and its many dimensions. Insatiable quests drive us in the thirst to learn and expand in awareness.

The insatiable quest requires adaptation and change. We are constantly in flux and never static. Our world always evolves into new forms or ideas. On a physical level, we are changing into new beings about every eighteen months (depending on the source). Every cell in our bodies has given birth to another cell, and cells die. No day, night, or moment is identical.

The anxiety we feel is based in fear. The range of intensity is from minor discomfort to panic or rage. It is anxiety that urges us to express ourselves or move our body.

Intolerance to change creates anxiety. As humans, we wish life would stand still for us. We feel comfortable and live in the past. It is a human desire to hold on to what no longer exists.

Change is the essence of the universal Creator. His Love expands the universe. We observe this growth in science. Imagine if we were never conceived because conception is a change from a single egg and a single sperm, which both were created from change to create change. We call this life. Science says identical twins are just that, yet are they? There is always some minute difference in their appearance or behavior, a way of telling them apart with good overt and covert observation.

Passion is an insatiable quest to accomplish something in a specific field, endeavor, or relationship. If we have one passion, we are fortunate. To have passion in our careers or relationships yields satisfaction and contentment in life. It is an insatiable quest to find who we are and what we aspire to achieve. It is possible to experience more than just one passion in a lifetime. This passion holds desire. There is more to the individual than one passion. This passion may expand linearly in creativity or be multidimensional.

The insatiable quest on earth starts with goals we wish to achieve for spiritual growth, and it ends with an easier death. We know that we have finished all we have sought to achieve in this lifetime. We have left behind loved ones who create their own passages in this world, and we have achieved our spiritual goals.

"Soar higher than eagles,
Glide faster than kites.
Fly past the present,
Into the future.
Fly into dreamland,
Wisp away into heaven.
The sun stirs my sleeping soul,
And wakens my body.
Dreams have vanished,
Into clouds forgotten.
Songs, sing his praise,
Angels whisper his name.
Dreams have vanished,
Into clouds forgotten.
Where am I in this dream?
I am here, I cried.
Dreams have vanished,
Into clouds forgotten."
—Bandit, Siberian husky

Chapter 23

Invasion

Home consisted of my husband, one child, and me. Then came the animals and caged birds—each with their own personalities. At first, it was a silent world of fur and feathers and the intermittent familiar dog, cat, and bird sounds. The world changed with our interpretations of their body language. What did they mean or want by this tail wag? We needed to figure them out. We had never-ending questions about their behavior.

This did a 180-degree turn with the knowledge of how to listen telepathically, thought transference from on being to another. Now we had a clear understanding that went beyond animal behavior. Their insight, knowledge, and awareness expounded in ways that expanded my world with their wisdom. To truly interact with them broadened our insight of what it is to be sentient in a world where vocal cords were not changed to produce verbal language.

Now our home is an empty nest with just the four of us: Henry, me, a Yorkshire terrier, and a domestic shorthair cat. We telepathically express ourselves, with our wants or needs; four voices, four personalities, and four sentient beings.

I often think back to the "old days." Would I want it to be that way again? No. Life now has meaning beyond myself. Thank goodness for the lost archaic moments of what they want. Life has become a clear communication of individual dreams, wishes, and daily insights in our family of four. Compromise has become a common word in our family.

It took a little practice to learn animal communication. What are you asking or saying? Their voices are easily heard and are loud and clear. One-way communication has turned into conversations between the four of us. The questions of seeking an understanding have vaporized into wondrous insight from animals and birds that are connected as true spirits to God. Hearing animals say their prayers makes my heart leap with gratitude. Gentle tears form in my eyes.

Cat Talk

There was a cat,
She was sassy,
She was batty.
She walked softly,
She stalked quietly,
She pounced briskly.
Cat of the field,
Cat in the house,
Cat catching mouse.
There was a cat,
She was sassy,
She was batty.

Chapter 24

Orange Dreams

"Dandelion paws" is what I say to Foxx. His Siberian husky body is entirely white. His paws are a sunny-side up yellow from running across the field dotted with yellow buttons. His feet look like my yellow face when I rub my cheek with a dandelion button. Every spring, Foxx enjoys running in the park. The dandelion buttons leave their yellow color on his paws and make him look like he has yellow rain boots on. Foxx's favorite color is yellow. Does he think of his feet wearing yellow mittens as he stands there proudly showing them off to me? He enjoys this moment with a silly grin.

I love sitting on a boulder and watching Foxx run on a spring morning. He has presence and a way about him that commands attention. He is regal without arrogance or pretense.

Two flat wooden sticks protrude from the small white bag I am holding. The bag is freezing as my thumbs find the indent and my fingers find the opposite side of the indent. The indent gives way in a soft crunch as my hands split the frozen popsicle into two halves. I pull on the paper. The paper releases a long, slender column of orange. Orange has a recognizable fragrance. How does one describe orange without using the word orange? A mix of yellow and red doesn't really do it. Yellow for the sun that brings life, and red is the passion in life. Yes, the orange of this old-time treat is the same orange and smell of my youth of warm summer days. My grandma would give me a nickel to buy something at the corner grocery store. As a little girl, I would hold the coin in my right hand and walk all the way to the store.

I walked three long blocks in the summer sun and up five steps to open the peeling green painted door into Meshke's corner grocery. The window signs were painted in an array of colors, advertising this week's specials. The grocery was one small room filled with baked goodies loaded with icing, canned goods, a meat counter, baskets of penny candy in all colors and flavors, and a freezer filled with ice cream wonders. There were many items packed tightly and neatly on the shelves.

I would hear Mr. Meshke pounding his cleaver through meat on a butcher block just beyond the back room doorway from the cash register. I raised myself onto my highest tiptoes to look over the counter. This time, he was butchering beef and grinding it up.

Mr. Meshke was a tall, thin, old man. He turned with a smile and a warm hello. He treated me nicely as if I was any of the grown-up people who came into his store. "What would you like?" He leaned over the counter and looked down to where I was standing. My choice was between my two favorites: orange or banana. Sometimes root beer was good too. I wondered why the company couldn't make half of each flavor into one popsicle. "Orange, please," I said with a grin. I held my hand high in the air to hand Mr. Meshke my nickel as he handed me my popsicle. The popsicle was cold and misty when it touched the warm summer air.

I thanked Mr. Meshke and headed home, unwrapping and folding the paper down around the wooden stick to catch the drips from the frozen treat. I walked slowly, pushing the popsicle in and out of my mouth with my tongue. It melted in my mouth, my tongue turned orange, and my nose filled with the smell of a real oranges. Sometimes I would slowly bite into the frozen crystals and softly crunch a small piece to melt away in my mouth. My fingers would stick to each other from the orange drips. How delicious. I was careful not to drip orange dots on my summer white pinafore. I did not want to get scolded when I got home for making a mess on my dress.

The color orange and the scent of a freshly peeled orange delight me. My life has encountered orange in all its abundance throughout my growing years: orange pop, ice cream, sherbet, candy orange slices, marshmallow peanuts, sunsets, flowers, and painted rooms. An era of hot pink and tangerine orange—and now tangerine orange is popular again for the summer. Best of all was the one-piece jumpsuit with its scooped-neck tank top and boy-cut short legs—terrycloth orange and comfortable.

My thoughts wandered to a lost memory. Years ago, in the summer, I was scheduled to teach baton and acrobatics to the high school band's front-line baton twirlers. One evening, I took a portable black-and-white television and put it in the teacher's lounge. A very popular weekly series was on, and I wanted to watch it while waiting for my ride home. I wore the orange jumper.

I had professionally taught the art of dance in my own studios when I was in high school. I looked forward to the class ending, knowing the television was waiting for me in the lounge.

The class ended, and every girl left chattering and giggling as usual as they went out the gym door. I put the mats away, packed the portable stereo, and gathered my things. The evening was sultry and filled with dampness. My hair naturally curls in high humidity, and with the workout, it was dripping down my cheeks. My bare feet felt the cool tile underneath as I romped down the empty hallway. I reminded myself that I could sit in the teacher's lounge on a cold vinyl chair and watch the TV show.

The teacher's lounge was only a couple of doors down on my right. I was feeling energetic from the evening's lesson. I swung open the door and leaped through the door, landing on my right foot. My eyes scanned the room in terror, noticing slick hair and the scent of Vitalis and Old Spice. A group of men filled the chairs around the walls. They turned and stared at me in surprise. I leaped back out and let the door shut behind me.

I went back to see if everyone had left the lounge. The room was empty. I wrapped the cord around the television and carried it to the car. Oh, my, oh my! What had I leaped into?

The answer came a few months later during a telephone call. My orange jumper and barefoot me had leaped into a school board meeting. I really felt like the lady coming out of the cake at a party. It took a while to get over the churning in the pit of my stomach. The bandleader (my husband) smiled as I explained the episode and gulped my way through it. It took longer for my dropped mouth to turn itself into a memory—and many years until I could laugh.

It is nice to sit here on this boulder, feel the summer breeze against my face, and finish my orange popsicle. A pleasant day off from work allowed my mind to wander.

I work as a registered nurse. Every day at work is an endeavor of keeping calm and helpful throughout my shift. I leave the hospital with a sense of satisfaction. Maybe someone is more comfortable than when I arrived.

Memories wander and drift in and out of my mind. Does the endless chatter of the mind ever stop? Sitting in the sun has a way of doing that. The memory was about a chance meeting with a doctor. I had briefly noticed him when he turned the corner past the nurse's station during his rounds. I had never worked with him. There are more than 120 specialists from the clinic at the hospital.

The doctor was in his sixties. He was tall, pleasant, and quiet. His personality implied he was a good family man, husband, and parent. It was easy to envision him reading a newspaper in an overstuffed chair with an Irish setter beside him. When he made his morning rounds, the nurses would say, "Just a nice guy—there could not be anyone nicer."

One day, he told me that he had noticed me for the past few months without saying a word. Today, he found the courage.

Courage for what? It all seems strange. My eyebrows crossed for a moment, and I smiled.

"I am older, and in my profession, I have seen a lot of women. I saw you working this floor and thought you looked so elegant and expensive. I was afraid to speak to you. I am finally glad that I did. After talking with you, I realize what an unpretentious and genuine person you are. If a man asked you out on a date, you would be tickled pink just to sit on a park bench, eat a hot dog, and enjoy his company. You are different than I imagined you to be. I am pleased to have met you."

That was that, and I did not see him after our short conversation. He seemed to have vanished.

He had paid me the highest compliment I had ever received. It was a compliment from a total stranger and totally unexpected. I stood there with a blank expression, nodded, smiled, and quietly thanked him. It was unexpected and a joyful insight to see a stranger take note of who I felt to be inside. He made me feel proud of my life and my work.

Would there be a man in my life who would seek the inner me and share my life with me? Would he enjoy sharing a hot dog or the other half of a melt-in-your-mouth orange popsicle? Would he understand my desires, needs, and dreams?

Would he know that I love walking through the pine trees? I caress the delicate white blossoms of the dogwood flower while infusing my nostrils with the honeysuckle fragrance released by the warmth of the morning sun. Would he have insight into the feeling of our being a miracle, vulnerable to the vastness of the universe we live in? The moonbeams softly light our faces as we gaze up into the stars and witness the magnitude of God.

Would this man share the coziness of feeling the warmth of Foxx's fur as we snuggle in bed with our heads on one pillow? Would he know my wonderment of faeries? Would he witness the beauty of life's most precious miracles? To spontaneously reveal a glistening smile, turning joy into laughter. To look deeply into his eyes as they sparkle gold and wonder what he sees in mine? To explore the excitement in searching the depths of each other's souls, knowing the completeness of love. Is there a man among the stars who reflects the light of my orange dreams?

"Together, we are one,
Together, we are hope.
Together, we are one,
Together, we are joy.
Together, we are one,
Together, we are love."
—Charles, white-tailed deer

Chapter 25

The Three Ps

Patterns

Fibonacci sequence is comprised of the Fibonacci numbers: 1, 1, 2, 3, 5, 8, 13, 21—an unending sequence where each term is defined as the sum of its two predecessors. We observe it all the time in nature without a second thought. One style, three stamen, and five petals—the number sequence feels right and in perspective.

Decorate a room with an odd number of the same or different objects, and it looks pleasing to the eye. The comfort level is in the odd number. In nature, patterns are everywhere.

Notice the beauty in the symmetrical human face, the ratios. The beauty in nature is with its natural symmetry and symmetrical values. Ever observe a mother with her newborn counting every finger and toe? All these feelings are inspired by nature. A mandala has symmetry with its center for focusing into meditation. It inspires us to seek the center of our divine hearts and connect to God.

Why did I write this? God created the patterns, and He created us. It is just an encouragement to learn what in nature inspires you. What patterns make you feel comfortable? What colors or shapes draw your attention to the design or impact of tones and shades in the different pigments? Is it a search to know more about our insights and our connections to our world and our preferences? We do not randomly choose our clothes each morning. Our subconscious chooses our need for the day in the clothes grabbed out of the closet. There is an inner complexity to color, design, inner feeling, impacting our moods and what we create about ourselves.

Our bodies have chakras. These spheres of energy have patterns and different colors that impact our lives, energy, and relationships. There is nothing in our bodies or our lives that is not impacted by design, color, vibration, or energy. Colors emitted from our bodies may show stress or health.

Ever tell someone they look pale? Does a person look depressed or blue? Is there infection, humiliation, or anger shown by a red face? Fingerprints, DNA, and questions arise—and we have the instinct to evaluate and prevail with accurate assessment in the patterns. Observe and enjoy!

Progeny

The outcome of our lives begins with each breath. Each breath is a moment to consider what we bring forth into our world.

It is difficult to create change in ourselves or others, yet we try. The opportunity exists in each moment. How can we make it different and become aware of what we are feeling before we respond?

A wonderful place to start is with a tiny sigh, a moment of reflection before making a final decision to speak or act. Before responding, ask if it be offered in kindness. Is the response given in calmness? Does the response offer compassion? Does the response create change in oneself or others? Am I able to create the change in myself and create the change around me? Does this change ripple outward and affect others or the environment?

Fleeting moments of spontaneous insight give rise to new and different outcomes. We aspire to positive outcomes, changing into a feeling of wellness, balance, and increasing our energy. This positive change offers the individual we seek to be in each moment in the journey home.

The word home is an intriguing word with wonderful insight. Home imparts the feeling of goodness and safety. Home has the two middle letters o and m. OM is the sound of God. In the moment of reflection before we speak or act, we go home for a moment. Home is in our heart. The fireplace is the heart of the home. It is where our heart is fired for each beat. In this moment, we are aware that we are offering ourselves in sincere kindness and compassion to others. A sigh takes us there.

When elderly people speak of going home, they are not talking about going home to a residential address. God is home. Home is where the heart is! It beats on earth and soars in heaven.

Promises

"Promises, promises, promises!" This is a lament of despair. Do we fulfill our promises or do we leave them unattended?

A promise is a promise. Do we still expect people to keep their promises? Do we keep our promises to others?

A promise honored is a joy of rainbow bubbles that elevates the heart.

A promise that remains unfulfilled bursts the bubble of respect for others. Always remember how you made them feel.

I promise you that I hold you dear in my heart for we are all his children.

"Where art thou? Where art Thou?
In your soul, in your soul.
Where art Thou? Where art Thou?
In your heart, in your heart.
Where art Thou? Where art Thou?
In your dreams, in your dreams."
—Spooky, pit bull

Chapter 26

Reflections of Spirit

My heart beats in the chaotic world around me. The journey of life is to return home to God, doing the best we can in any given moment. The physical journey between birth and death is chaotic. Its growing pains are sorrowful, painful, and joyful. Chaos can yield to frustration, depression, and anger. A rainbow of emotions leads my feet through life. The emotions bound my heart to beat at an even keel or a frantic race.

The mind, the thinker, and the believer portray the ego pushing and shoving me about in this world. I am frantic and frustrated at the constant jumbled, nonsensical chatter that rambles in my mind. Belief reflects doubt and uncertainty. It tries to lead the way to decisions and control of me. Push me, pull me—which way do I go?

Life is a journey—not a path. A path winds and may even circle back on itself. One can be on or off a path, walk backward on a path, go in circles on a path, sit down, or camp out on a path. Our journey creates the destination. A journey is always in the present moment and is lived in the current moment. It moves forward in a constant progression. The journey has a destination to return from whence we came, heaven.

How do I know I am in the present? In the present, I observe a situation from a nonjudgmental perspective of comparison. This innocent perception has insight and wisdom when I do not inflict judgment, create a past of comparison, or a future of nonexistent wishes. The present is a gift from God. Enjoy and love the moment. Experience it in observations or feelings. I remember dressing my toddler in cute clothes. This past does not exist. I enjoy and love my teenager as a magnificent, breathing being in front of me now. That does exist. Comparison and judgment are nonexistent in the now. Every nanosecond, a microscopic event in time, is all we have.

The heart is the emotion, the feeling, inner instinct, and the knowing soul as the perfection of God. I allow my life to flow like a river from the mouth to its source—from me to God. I remember to ask, ask, and ask again: Which way, dear God, which way do I go? What should I do? It takes a miniscule moment to ask and receive the answer.

Will my heart create beauty in this chaos of life? Yes. I already know everything has been created and exists right now. I ask for my heart's desire and guidance. It was created before I asked. It already exists. My heart received the blessing of God. He gave me what I asked for in his own way—in his own time. Gratitude is thankfulness to the Creator. He has created what I have asked, and it has been given. God wants me to have abundance in all aspects of life. He loves me unconditionally and wants me to live in joy. Ask, know, and gratitude are the true words of trinity for creating and manifesting in life.

Chaos tells me that I am an individual. Yes, I am that. I am that I am. I have evolved to know my inner preferences. There is only one truth, and it comes from my direct connection with God. Others tell me that we will never be as One for we are each different as individuals. We are different in the preferences of our daily lives, our physical makeup, and our experiences. We are walking the same journey—at different paces—and are united in a common goal.

Some people say, "I believe that to be the truth for me." Others say, "I do not believe that. I believe this." Belief is the ego saying, "Me, me, me!"

At times, a comment comes from structured educational or religious organization to believe only what an institution designates as truth from their established criteria or by-laws. This is fine. They are functioning from a source other than questioning or seeking their own individual questions. They are where they are, and it is okay. Maybe they will progress spiritually in this life or a future life. Maybe something will be said that questions the truth of what they believe as individuals.

Whoa. How can this be? We honor another's individual awareness of unique progress to the attainment of knowing from the divine heart within.

There is only one truth: God's truth. His truth is Love. I am you, you are me, and we are all One in his name. Unity brings harmony to chaos. It is the knowing, the inner wisdom, and awareness of the connection to everyone and everything in this web of life. I love it when it is expressed by saying, "I know. I just know." Knowing comes from within our divine hearts. Spirituality is atonement. Atonement is the awareness that we are one with God and connect in the web of all life: atonement (at-one-ment). "Three things cannot be long hidden: the sun, the moon, and the truth." —Buddha

Chaos is created in the institution of religion. Masses of people believe differently and create a dogma for others to follow. My belief is the right way—the only way—and this creates division. If I expel or explode my beliefs onto other people, is this not my dogma, my religion, my life? Live spelled backward is evil. To live life away from our direct connection with God is evil and results in chaos.

To live life is living in God's will. It is not about personal choices or free will, slightly changing one's life script. It is as simple as to live or not live in the will of God. Living in God's will is to ask, know, and feel gratitude. One truth, the inner knowing, gives unity creating respect, honor, and unconditional love. Faith in him, his truth, creates harmony, the oneness.

Can individuals with different awareness of the progression of their spiritual journeys be brought together to celebrate life? Absolutely everyone is included in celebrating life when we show acceptance of others. Love leads the way through patience and nurturing the spiritual expression of who we are. Love is all there is and ever will be; it is eternal. Love is to surrender all expectations for myself and others—to live in grace and heartfelt gratitude. We move ourselves forward from living in the law of karma into the law of grace.

What about forgiveness? Is forgiveness an integral part of living in God's will? Is this the way to love myself and others? How can this be? Is forgiveness a judgment of comparison of myself and others? Judgment implies one of us is at fault. How can forgiveness lead to acceptance and love when it is based in judgment—an ego comparison founded in fear?

I asked, and He answered. Create two words! For and give is the response in gratitude from the heart, not a place of compassion. Responding in the positive, the result is expressing love with a thank you for giving me the opportunity to know you better, understand you, and unconditionally accept you as you are. It works! It comes from the heart, and it remains positive in sincerity. It offers love and subdues fear; neither lives in the same space and time as the other. It is not right or wrong. It is not a judgment of oneself or another. It is what works or does not work. It is a learning experience given among the opportunity of chaos. For giving love has a positive outcome for change.

My breath is my gratitude, my love, and inspiration for knowing who I am. I AM Him. He is the infinite particle that is in all spaces, the connection, and the all-knowing Oneness. He gives me learning experiences in life to let go of the ego mind and live in the heart of love. To use my mind as a tool for which it was created—two plus two is four. I reflect in spirit within my heart. The answer lies there. He is my divine heart.

My journey and spirituality are represented in the cross. The original cross was created in blue and green. Blue is the spiritual, the vertical from earth/creation (us) upward to heaven (God), and green is the horizontal journey from birth to death (from left to right, a journey). Blue is etheric, and green is physical.

The sign of the cross is eternity expressed with love. When people cross themselves or others, it starts at the holy eye (the bright area of light within us where God placed the Holy Spirit is observed during meditation). It moves vertically downward from the Holy eye and stops at the divine heart (a heart behind the physical heart, a heart space called the zero point, the void where God resides within us). The horizontal motion is from the widest part of our bodies, our shoulders. Start by pointing to the left shoulder and move across the chest to the right shoulder. When crossing another or an object, it is performed in the opposite way. From birth (mother: feminine is left side of the body, into this physical world) to death/transformation across the chest is our journey through life into heaven (father: masculine is right side of the body, power, into the etheric world).

The sign of the cross was changed in earth's history from Father, Son, and Holy Mother to Father, Son, and Holy Ghost possibly due to a chauvinistic religious society denying feminine equality. Our Blessed Mother is the matrix. What one believes from upbringing holds precedence for them. As one grows spiritually, with an open mind and heart, this concept may change. Many concepts will change and evolve in the Second Coming. The Second Coming is about mankind evolving spiritually. Nothing in life is status quo. Humanity anticipates or comes kicking and screaming into evolution. This has occurred throughout history.

"Bow ties are the fit of me,
Bow ties are the cool of me,
Bow ties are the gist of me.
Bow ties are the smile in me,
Bow ties are the laugh in me,
Bow ties are the joy in me.
Bow ties are the part of me,
Bow ties are the smart of me,
Bow ties are the fun of me."
—Milton, dachshund

Chapter 27

Sands of Time

November 11, 2011 arrives on a Friday. It is Veterans Day. Why is this significant? This year the numbers are in trinity with the number 11-11-11. In numerology, the sacred numbers are eleven (highest or holiest), twenty-two, and thirty-three. If you add the number of your birth (5-29-1965), the birth month and day are totaled and reduced and is the same for the year. The month and day is added 5+2+9=16–1+6=7, the year is added 1+9+6+5=21–2+1=3.

The sacred numbers are never reduced or counted. Therefore, eleven is a holy number, a holy day, and a day of high vibration. Each day holds the number eleven on the clock twice: 11:11 a.m. and 11:11 p.m.

Veterans Day in our school years meant facing east at eleven in the morning with our right hands placed over our hearts. The town's whistle blew at 11:00 a.m. on Veterans Day (it also blew at noon to reset our clocks or for a weather warning), and the people of our country stood in silence to honor soldiers and veterans. Prayer was an option. We still have veterans who are coming home with the honor of our country: the loss of life. A minute each year for these patriots and historic patriots is the tiniest speck of time. "Thank you! I am free because of you, your patriotism, and courage." I stood proudly facing the east and still do. My grandmother always said that the saddest of all moments in life is hearing the trumpet sounds in a cemetery to honor a fallen soldier. Our hearts cry outward, and tears drip down our cheeks at the lonely sound of Taps.

I am grateful that our soldiers—with the support of their

families—cared enough about this country and its people to put their lives on the line to keep freedom and democracy in the USA. A soldier's bravery and endurance is beyond my comprehension or imagination. When the school system or government abolished this ritual of honor, I felt as if something within my heart was missing. We have lost something sacred. I invite you to stand with me to face east on Veterans Day for one minute to honor those patriots who still live or died in service.

You may light two white candles to represent the number eleven. The candle flames draw upon air to be lit as we draw in air for life. This quiet celebration is a reflection of our lives in relationship to the Creator who our heroes return to. Spirits can see a candle flame—not the light from electric light bulbs. It is a moment to honor another. I see you in me. You are me, and I am you.

The date signifies the Four-Corner vortex that appears every 26,000 years. The vortex will last one to two years, releasing the negative energy from the earth. The Four Corners connect Arizona, New Mexico, Colorado, and Utah. For those fortunate to be present during this vortex, it offers the opportunity to experience it, feel the high vibration, and communicate or message with the Creator. A vortex is a life-changing spiritual experience that connects with the Creator and creation through prayer, meditation, and ritual.

This is a sacred era for humanity. The solar logo is a cleansing of human negativity and spiritual awakening to live in unity with the Christ consciousness. The Second Coming has begun. Our Lord is present. A new heart-world of unifying consciousness awaits us to live in compassion, honor, and respect in the oneness with the ever-present all.

The infusion of psychic children continues. They are children who have never lived on earth. They are called the Genesis Children. The completion of the Second Coming takes twenty-five years. The change is coming for all—a kind new world living in the law of grace. My prayers are with everyone during their spiritual journeys as they walk with love and gratitude.

Karen Kober

Salute

You fought for our county,
With patriotism and bravery,
Holding strong and steadfast,
Keeping our flag held high.
You fought for our country,
Holding head up with pride,
Justice and loyalty steadfast,
Family and country back home.
You fought for your country,
Standing tall with courage,
Freedom strong and steadfast,
Your faith led you back home.
Bravery is courage uncloaked.
The preservation of freedom,
Tolls the liberty bell.

Chapter 28

Shine

The term psychic is the knowing/intuition of the unseen. It is the spiritual ability to live in the earth realm and communicate telepathically from the spirit world. It is demonstrated by a vibration connection to the oneness. Psychic can be broken down into two parts: psychic/spiritual or psychic/evil. Psychic and spiritual are defined in the dictionary with the same definition. When one grows spiritually, one grows psychically too.

Light workers are people who are spiritual in their connection to the Light of God. Their work and relationships with others have compassion and ethical values. Their lights shine from God through themselves to others. It is a blessing to know these individuals. A new generation of children—the Genesis Children—are being born into this earth as advanced light workers. Light workers have enlightened abilities that create peace within their beings and emit a presence of peace in others. Their work is honest, respectful, and has integrity while offering dignity.

Light workers live the joy with sacredness within their hearts. Evil is living life away from God. Free will is the choice to live life with God or away from Him . There are beings that enter this life void of human emotions. Psychic/evil works lack integrity, honesty, and respect. It is about the victory over other souls.

Does everyone have psychic abilities? Yes. All humans have psychic abilities. The difference between the psychic/light and psychic/evil is having a conscience or not. One has the ability to love or have guilt/remorse, and the other does not. Psychic/evil are the people who scam/con/commit crimes or kill (vile is the four letter word from live here). One has to acknowledge that the difference does exist. It cannot be implied that a minute spark of God exists in every human who lives an evil life. It does not; it may be totally absent.

It is beneficial to ask God before dealing with anyone whether they are of the light or darkness. Darkness is deceptive. The malicious intent of falsehoods and manipulation is embedded with intelligence and charisma. It is the ultimate con. Everyone can be charmed or fooled. To think that one cannot be is a dangerous concept. Many are in jail, yet others are in society. We are all vulnerable to them. There is no prison or psychiatric ward that can contain a sociopath. They escape. There are many symptoms and signs of sociopaths. It is easy to spot a sociopathic personality. It sends up an internal red flag that something is amiss. Remove yourself from the person or situation as delicately as possible.

Living with the positive aspects of interacting with others is fulfilling. If there is a dangerous situation involving another, it is not easy to pass by without being involved. One is present in the situation for a purpose, and that is to intervene as best as one can. I cannot and will not allow verbal, physical, emotional, or mental abuse of another adult, child, or animal. At times, it creates jeopardy for me. Institutions or personal situations feel threatened when people stand their ground to honor God within themselves or others.

I always felt that the R in RN meant respectful and responsible nurse. In the long run, I cannot do anything differently in my life. I do not look the other way. It is not the God within me to ignore another's plight. Some may call it foolhardy or courageous. I may not judge others for the decision to choose personal action or inaction. Please do not confuse observation and judgment; they are not the same.

Life is pleasant in the light. Sometimes it means seclusion to promote inner peace against dealing with the world of chaos. Sometimes it means releasing people who are causing chaos from their respective points in the journey. Release them with blessing; your lesson and their lesson are over. It is time for each one to move forward separately.

Yeshua says, "Divorce and death end a marriage." They have

accomplished the learning needs they agreed upon in spirit before entering their bodies. Bless them on their journeys and move forward. This may not only involve a marriage; it may be a friendship or a family relationship.

Life is so much easier when everything is turned over to God. It becomes the worn phrase: "Let go and let God." Easier said than done? It is easier to let go and allow the next moment to be happier. The light within us is sacred, and the light of God will shine forth. This light will shine in our world to evolve into a compassionate place to live together. The future holds promise and hope when it is lived with compassion.

"Hope expands from one to all,
Love encompasses his all.
Peace provides the companionship,
Joy rejoices from his sweet call."
—Donali, cardinal

"Pretty as a princess,
Pretty as a pink bow,
Pretty as a pink rose.
Pretty says and read prose,
Pretty to rise and to bed,
Pretty to sigh and yearn.
Pretty is who I am,
Pretty is love in bloom,
Pretty is who I am."
—Monroe, dachshund

Chapter 29

Soul or Spirit?

The soul is a physical vessel. In this form, we have memories, dreams, feelings, creations, and emotions. The journey to the womb goes through the tunnel from heaven. A bend in the tunnel makes us forget our experiences in heaven. We try to hang on to them, very few succeed. Most of us only have inklings.

On earth, we journey to remember our spiritual/psychic lessons as we head home through the tunnel to return to God, heaven, family, and friends. The soul in etheric form may remain on earth (there is no crossing over) to heal any unresolved issues. If we experience a sudden death and the conscience is not aware the body died, we call this existence a ghost.

A spirit crosses over and comes back from heaven to visit loved ones. The spirit is entitled to attend its own funeral to witness the gathering of loved ones. Humans only gather in multitude for births and deaths. Spirits love being with their families at celebrations. The spirit is known to visit between three and four o'clock in the morning or during our dreams.

Spirits may choose to visit, appear at will, or invite a person to come home with them. When being invited home, it is the living one's choice to accept or decline. In heaven, we recognize everyone from this life and all past lives. There is a lot of catching up to do with what has happened after leaving for earth. New people who have returned home are easily spotted because they are constantly merging with each other to catch up on the latest news.

Spirits will show themselves as apparitions of how they appeared on earth so that you may recognize them. They may appear translucent or solid. We see them through the digital camera as wispy clouds, orbs, or human forms. Digital cameras allow us to view another dimension and see through the veil. Digital cameras show us another dimension. Microscopes and telescopes allowed us to view new horizons of knowledge when they were invented. At times, ghosts and spirits may be visible to the naked eye.

Are we spiritual or psychic when we use the natural gifts God embedded in each of us? Actually spiritual and psychic are synonyms. Growing closer to God is what we are here to accomplish. Sometimes this takes many lifetimes to learn. When we have completed the many tasks we desired to learn, we go home to God. It is a natural cycle, repeated through re-manifestation to grow spiritually faster by coming to earth. If we remained in heaven, we could accomplish the same goals—but the completion would take enormously longer. We are strong individuals to come to this earth.

What happens if we have not adjusted to our spirits being free again and back home in heaven? There is a period of readjustment to life back in heaven. There is a healing place, and many deceased people in spirit forms are assigned to help us with our reentry into heaven. What happens if we have been severely negative or harmful on earth? There is hope in the Second Coming since this period will be used for cleansing of these people.

In our usual return home, we are thirty again and in bodies we choose. Thirty is considered mature yet young. If we have not attained our goal of becoming closer to God and have remained away from Him in our negative/evil actions on earth, we walk in heaven as old. Others do not interact with them.

After the death of the physical body, there is a life review to give us insight into whether we succeeded in accomplishing our spiritual goals. An example would be Hitler. God wants all his children to come home to him. He denies no one. The difference is shown in our physical appearances. In the law of grace, there is a new law from God that we are accountable at all times for our actions and creations. I do not know what this entails, and I did not ask. I will walk in the light of God. What you choose to experience in the outcome in this new law will be between you and God. I do not think it will be favorable to those who ignore the presence of God in others or the earth.

Whatever form we are witnessing, soul or spirit, there is absolutely nothing to fear if we live in the will of God. When you feel uncomfortable or in doubt, your spirit must respond to two universal words: "back off." One may use the *Soak and Seal* for protection. The Soak and Seal is found for personal use in *www.divineheart. org*. Demonic entities may need another form to send them back. A person who is violated may need an exorcism. Priests are trained for this and care for everyone. One may feel more comfortable asking spirits to visit you in your dreams to relay messages they have for you. Most visits with us are loving opportunities to share the presence of a loved one.

The solar logo and the Second Coming began in the summer of 2011. Love and fear cannot occupy the same space or time. With love, we feel inner peace and compassion that unite us with each other and God's creations.

Yeshua comes for everyone to show us the way of life with love and without fear. Yeshua has asked the symbol for the Second Coming to be the lamb. He also wished to be called by the name He knows Himself to be: Yeshua. Bless all in His name.

Karen Kober

Yeshua

Joy is a jubilant feeling of love.
OM is the sound of Father God.
Yeshua is His Hebrew name.
Faith knows God is grace.
Unity is harmony in life.
Life is the beauty we walk.

Chapter 30

Stone Story

The searing heat of the beating sun made the black mare breathe warmly and slowly. Tewa ambled forward with a drooped head, mouth and body frothing from the heat. Anetonka, an Indian of many summers, sat astride Tewa. His Indian name, Anetonka, means running fox. As a young warrior, he could run as fast as a cunning fox.

The journey to return to his tribe was long and hard on Anetonka. His old body was lean and worn with only the memories of a strong, vital youth. A single white feather wrapped with a strip of buckskin was tied to the side of his long silver hair. He felt the scorching heat of the high Southwest sun on his bare shoulders. His body was tired and aching, and he sensed the fatigue in Tewa from her slowed movement.

The river was close, and Tewa snickered in her thirst for the water that filled her nostrils with a wet fragrance. The water glistened as they approached the river. The long river was between home and the Spanish-speaking people. Tewa instinctively headed for the water. She stopped with her front hooves at the waterline and lowered her head to drink the coolness.

As she drank, Anetonka swung down from the mare onto the embankment. The desert grass bent softly under his moccasins. He squatted and scooped a handful of water to drink. The cool water soothed the dry desert dust from his parched lips. His wet hands felt soothing as he rubbed them over his face. He lingered a moment to watch the water ripple and dance from a slight breeze and current. It was time to give Tewa a rest. It would take another moon to reach his tribe.

A small pack of wolves stood atop a high ridge, looking down at

Anetonka. The largest gray wolf, an alpha male, recognized Anetonka as the "Old Wise One" from the Chiricahau tribe of the Apache Nation. With respect for the honored two-legged, their paws gave no sound as they turned and disappeared back over the edge of the ridge.

Anetonka stood, stretched his hands high above his head, and felt the thirst of the trail. He squatted to scoop more water from the river. His hand passed over two river stones that caught his eye. The stones touched each other under the water's shallow edge. Over endless seasons under the fast current, the two stones had become worn and smooth. The stones reminded Anetonka of his worn body and his presence in the river of life.

The Old Wise One knew of the stone people, yet he was unaware the two stones were friends. The stones shared the bond of knowing the other was there as stone people do. Countless sunrises gave way to change in the life that surrounded them. They spun many a tale of what they had witnessed through the endless moments of river life. Each story gave them insight into new meanings and the soul of the other.

Anetonka, without knowing why, had an urge to pick up the two stones. He stood up and arched his back with his right hand on the back of his shoulder. He flung both stones at once over the glistening water. He watched them skip and splash into the water. The stones disappeared into the depths of the river. He had done this many times as a child. In his final years, his body felt the movement of skipping stones with his aching joints.

Oh, what agony surged through the stone people as they were flung high in the air above the river. What sadness, loneliness, and sorrow to be hurled away from each other. The stones felt the bottomless pit of primordial despair. They felt an empty loss as they sank into the black water as it lost the light of the sun in the increasing depth of the river. They realized simultaneously they would never know or touch each other again. They felt the unbearable void of solitude. The intense separation was as vast as the silent darkness of the river.

When the ripples touched, there was great rejoicing. The stone people found their spirits were in union. Each stone suddenly understood they were never separate or alone. They were One. Each stone knew Mother Earth would create a destiny for their love and friendship, returning them to each other again.

Star Child

Live a life of love.
Star child
Star of the night,
Star of the sea,
Shine bright white,
Shine unto thee.
Star of the night,
Star of the sea,
Give your light,
To his thy be.
Angel of the night,
Mermaid of the sea,
Unfold your light,
Shine unto thee.
Star of his mother,
There is only wonder,
Her eyes meet his,
A star beams yonder.
Starlight from yonder,
Holds the wonder,
Shines on Virgin Mother,
And her star child.

Chapter 31

Survivor

In spiritual or hypnosis sessions, some adults felt they survived childhood and youth experiences with unwanted demands placed upon them. They feared their parents, grandparents, or church belief systems. They felt conflicted about who they were. Their childhoods offered no opportunities to question family or church expectations about what and how they would live as adults on their spiritual journeys.

In our social and religious histories, parents, grandparents, and churches used fear to instill the dogma of an established institution's belief systems. Sensitive children are overwhelmed by the fear and control issues put upon them. "In raising you, you will live life as I/ we say, believing what I/we believe. What was good enough for my parents is good enough for you. You do as the church says or you will go to hell—or burn in hell."

This brainwashing occurs with the constant bombardment of someone else's belief system throughout childhood, as young adults, or even later in life. The guilt applies to children who do not follow the belief systems of their parents, grandparents, or churches. They will be living in sin, going to hell, or living in purgatory. The lack of opportunity to question, as children do with curious minds, leads to blindly following what they inwardly sense is not true for them. Is it right that they are told not to question what is and always has been? Sensitive children have difficulty coping, fear doing something wrong, and feel unworthy of love.

Information is disseminated from family members who incorporated their beliefs without questioning the truth of their dogma. Without verbalizing it, sensitive children question what they are feeling or misunderstanding. It is as it is.

Years of resentment turn into anger. They have no choice. How could they do this to me? As adults, they find resolution or reflection of the feelings that corrupt their lives. They express themselves as victims. They display emotional fear and resentment. To release the victimization, they seek what feels good and comfortable through inner compassion of who they are.

Adults seek psychiatrists, psychologists, or hypnotists to release fear, anger, and resentment, which includes feelings of lack of worth and power or lowered self-esteem. Without release, their childhood experiences remain present in their adult lives, affecting relationships, families, and careers.

How do they move forward without the past clinging to their lives? How do they release it? Are they able to release pent-up negative emotions? Thinking they are able to self-release their emotions is temporary at best. The emotions have a way of creeping right back into their daily lives. The anger and fear never seem to dissipate. The recommended ways appear futile and negative. It is implied that one needs to forgive all involved and move forward. This action seems lost in judgment of oneself—or others—that something they or others did was wrong. The outcome remains negative and unresolved.

The negative is fraught with inner feelings of guilt. To create a positive outcome of living and being constantly aware of what one is feeling creates a choice for change. This works by checking their personal emotions in the present moment and sensing what their emotions are expressing. Leaving past experiences of imposed adult authoritarian dogma and religious experiences with parents, grandparents, or church is their issue. It was their way. It is to be honored. It was the best they could do. It was promoted by centuries of expectations from religious institutions and culture.

Can living life in gratitude resolve the conflict of dogma versus personal spirituality? Yes, gratitude holds the key to acknowledging that our pasts created the unique individuals we are today.

Spirituality is a personal and intimate connection with God. Spirituality does not need an interpreter or a third party, such as family or clergy, to tell them what to believe. They already know within themselves. Can one live in dogma and be spiritual? Yes. There are many who have done so for themselves. It was what they knew in their hearts that yielded the connection to God and life. Before we entered life on earth, we chose our parents for the experience we wished to learn. We wrote our learning experiences into scripts before we entered our lives. This was a self-imposed negative learning experience to grow spiritually—a way to feel whole and balanced in daily living.

In gratitude, we grow spiritually from this background of negativity into positive emotions. We learn who we are and what our journeys are about. It is the old-fashioned quip: God bless them. Yes, bless your family for their fortitude of their religious institutional rituals. It felt right to them. They felt no need to question because they believed this is the way it has always been. Why change it? Parents were in a place of comfort and security in following the masses. It is okay for them. Is it okay to grow spiritually in your journey? Yes!

The imposition from family about what one should believe often leaves people feeling something is missing. We are whole and perfect in the eyes of God. Honor who you are and the life you live. We all do the best we can in any given moment.

View the childhood experience of a rigid upbringing as positive because it created who you are today. One has a greater understanding of life being about love and what one can do for mankind. Our lives are about releasing inner turmoil. Change this turmoil from past negative and leave it in the past. Now is the time for a positive, fulfilling life. Honor the roles your family played in your personal life. They did what they did because they loved you. Know that you chose this upbringing to learn there is always a choice in every moment. To live every moment in the present gives clarity to joy. It is the proverbial expression of your cup being half full. I invite you to a full cup of positive living. God loves you—and so do I.

Tomorrow Never Is

Tomorrow never is,
Yesterday never was,
Today is here, right now.
Tomorrow is only dreams,
Yesterday only memories,
Today are memories to dream.
Tomorrow is a promise,
Yesterday is illusion past,
Today is here, this moment.
Survivor
Say it again, I am_____ and I am a survivor!

Chapter 32

The Greater More

What secret? Was there ever a secret? No, probably not. Do we wish for the magic in life? Can we attain the miracles? Can we manifest our desires? What is our purpose on earth?

We ask ourselves so many questions. There must be something more—a Greater More—than our everyday lives. The Greater More has always been there, yet we often suppress it—and so do organized institutions. We allow others to think for us. It comes from the Greater More to question and independently seek the truth for oneself. The truth is already within us. Our inner knowing is the true secret of our eternal connection with the Greater More.

We have always been aware of the answers within our divine hearts. The secret of knowing is as old as humankind. Whatever name one calls this Greater More, it matters not—as long as the name resonates within you.

The Greater More is our Creator, and our Creator is the unifying consciousness within ourselves that connects us to everyone and everything. This in its entirety is called oneness or the web of life.

The recognition is that the Greater More works through the subconscious to surface in our consciousness. This is where the magic of miracles occurs as we strive to manifest the miracles of our inner desires.

Our purpose from birth to our return home is to relearn this specific awareness of the Greater More. You and I are one with all creation. There is no place in the universe where the Greater More is not. The Greater More resonates in love, joy, kindness, honesty, respect, generosity, and compassion.

Happiness and joy is the true secret. We are joy, we radiate joy, we express joy, and we are the Greater More. Our inner children still find it fun to wish upon a star!

Holds Promise

The journey holds promise,
The journey holds experience,
The journey holds awareness,
The journey holds you and me,
The journey holds only our love.
The cycle of loving never ends,
The cycle of dreaming never ends,
The cycle of learning never ends,
The cycle of knowing never ends,
The cycle of being never ends.
The promise is eternal,
The promise is a whisper,
The promise is our love,
The promise is our life,
The promise is our God.

Chapter 33

One - Two - Three

"We danced all night." Waltzing in the New Year is uplifting to our hearts and spirit. To dance and hold each other is easily lost in movement and tempo. To swirl and sway to a melodic melody transcends one's mind into a fluid dream world. Dancing engages a moment to share in the oneness with a partner of special meaning. A New Year's Eve kiss may offer an alternative, yet dancing entwines holding each other in dreams, hopes, and possibilities.

A New Year's promise changes something in our lives that we feel we need to correct or aspire to. Our resolutions fade into a reality of promises not kept. It is fun to make a resolution list each year and hope for the best. Our hopes, desires, and dreams are better than we are. We honor ourselves for a better tomorrow, yet tomorrow never comes. The first day of the New Year inspires us to hope and dream about our goals and anticipated accomplishments for the year ahead.

Would it be easier to take our resolutions in small hops rather than a giant leap by reaching a simple daily goal for each day? There are a lot of pieces of chocolate in the candy box. One can only savor one piece at a time. A simple resolution may inspire one to stop and enjoy each piece of chocolate, savor it, making a simple resolution attainable. Every dance has many steps, and each step leads into the next step to create a waltz.

The first wedding waltz with your life partner or the bride with her father initiates a new beginning of well wishes of the couple's journey dancing as one. The wedding waltz is celebrated each year as an anniversary waltz. Dance or cuddle in the music and share the memories of the past and dreams for the future. Many a waltz played through the big band era and into our hearts.

One floats with the music about the dance floor without a single thought of how to waltz. One knows inside that it is easy and simple to dance with one's heart. Keeping our lives simple makes life easier. The end of the dance is the inner joy and a thank you to your partner for sharing a beautiful and magical waltz held in each other's arms over a lifetime of living. Dancing down memory lane, counting the waltz steps, and wishing every dance brings the promises of our dreams coming true. Dancing as a couple, supporting each other in our arms, and living the oneness in dancing is a spiritual experience.

"Winding my way through your heart,
Lost in your heart, breath, and thoughts.
Winding my way through your heart,
Longing of desires and foolish wishes.
Winding my way through your heart,
Seeking your embrace and listening heart."
—Teddy, retriever

Chapter 34

Open Window

An open window brings the vastness of the outside world to our senses. An open window entices us to expand our views and knowledge. Our Holy eye, like an open window, allows a vision of what is truly within ourselves, others, and the world around us. Accepting what we perceive in our reality is overt (obvious) and covert (hidden) observation.

Observation is neutral and holds no consequences. Why is it not a judgment? A judgment is when we put an ethical value on what is observed. A judgment is applied to the action—and not the person. Is little Johnny naughty—or is his action naughty? Do I admonish Johnny or the behavior? Johnny's behavior holds consequence, this is how we learn and grow.

Our interpretation of the world through the open window is reflected in our senses. The window provides an opportunity for awareness that we are connected to everything and everyone outside of ourselves. Am I alone when I peer through the open window? Or am I joined in oneness and the awesomeness of God's creation? I am no longer alone when I hear the birds singing, see the breeze sway the leaves of a tree, and smell the freshness and sweetness in the air. I am incorporated into the peace of the oneness of life. We are easily swayed to become lost in the trance of tranquility. Bringing tranquility into our lives becomes easier with a sigh and a drop of the shoulders before offering a response to another.

Through the open window I hear a siren and notice an ambulance blazing its way through traffic. I offered a silent prayer as the ambulance siren screams into the distance and fades away. Someday I will be carried in an ambulance and pray that you make way for me. Someday it may be you lying on this ambulance cart bound for the nearest emergency room. I am you, and you are me.

The children are yelling in the playground, singing their childhood chants. I have been them and must not forget that the child within me is still them. Dogs barking and children's noises are the sounds of life. I am grateful that I am here to experience these precious sounds. Life files through the open window.

My own heartbeat and breath fill this capsule with its own rhythm of life as I stand peering through this open window. My thoughts are rambling and endless. Some thoughts have purpose and others have no meaning. My thoughts, like my heartbeat and respirations, allow me to share life. As I look out of the open window I ponder the thoughts of the trees, grass, water in the stream, the rabbits and squirrels, flowers, and the stone path. What are their thoughts? What is life like for them? Consciousness is not only a human condition for everything is sentient because God created everything to be sentient.

It is easy for me to see in this dimension, and my Holy eye allows me a window to see into other dimensions. The families of the elf, fairy, and leprechaun are as busy in their worlds as I am in mine. I am in joy. There is an open window for me to observe life in many dimensions. We are all connected in creation. Join me and open the window to see me as I see you.

Karen Kober

"One heart, one beat,
Two hearts, two beats.
One is me, and one is you,
Two heartbeats into one heart.
One heart visible,
One heart is hidden.
Two hearts beating as One,
We are under the sun."
—Jack Russell terrier

Chapter 35

Rainbow Circle

The arched rainbow shows no beginning or end of the soft, delicate colors as it etches its way across the dark gray sky. A ribbon of God's colors—red, orange, yellow, green, blue, indigo, and purple—displays heartrending beauty. Two rainbows, one above the other, double the joy to witness. A sunbow is a rainbow of peaceful colors reflected in the moisture of the clouds surrounding the sun.

Rainbow colors are found in dewdrops, prisms, auras, and the chakras. I walked out on a winter morning and saw the rainbow's colors reflected from single crystals of snow. They were interspersed in the vastness of the white crystals of snowflakes. The unexpected bounty of God's colors sparkling across the snow gave a leap of gratitude to witness something I had never seen.

Energy fields of rainbow colors surround our bodies in an egg shape called an aura. The auras change color according to what is happening inside our emotions and our lives. Chakras are energy wheels that align in our bodies. Auras and chakras are from the rainbow. Each color has its own symbolic meaning. These colors reflect the physical, emotional, mental, and spiritual health of our souls.

Each chakra sends a cord from us to another person and from them to us. The thickness of the cord depends on the intensity of the relationship. The cords from one person connect with another person (and vice versa) even if the meeting is for a passing second. These cords show the health of our relationships with each other. If the chakra cord is positioned to an area other than the heart or is unhealthy in appearance, it can be repositioned for a healthy relationship or to sever the relationship.

God gives us his colors to observe in us and around us to let us know He is present. The rainbow symbolizes hope, the beginning of life, and an ending to symbolize the end of our journey and return home to heaven. The rainbow continues into the earth and back out and creates a complete circle. The rainbow circle on earth symbolizes the eternal love of God.

Rainbows often come after a period of darkness and are accompanied by rain. After the darkness, the sun brings forth the droplets of moisture in the rainbows. The color may have different intensities. Our lives reflect dark periods followed by light. God is showing us how the hope of light returns to our souls, spirits, and hearts.

A rainbow picture or painting is often accompanied by a white temple dove (a dove of peace). The temple dove has a soft beak and is the only bird that does not peck. When one witnesses a rainbow that arches over the top of a creature, one is seeing an incarnate angel in the form of a creature that was sent here to guide us. Sometime we see this in paintings; an example would be a white dove with a rainbow over it.

Each creature is a true spirit, and there is always in direct connection with God. A creature's physical need to have its body touch the earth is to feel God. This keeps them grounded and balanced in all aspects of physical, mental, emotional, and spiritual connections with Him. Earth creatures express telepathically that with the death of the physical body, the spirit goes over the rainbow bridge to return home to heaven and to God. It is the rainbow path to love.

Rainbows give us joy and peace. Our eyes glint with recognition of the beauty, and we smile at the rainbow. Our bodies sigh with inspiration. The rainbow colors are the colors of God. The rainbow is a promise from God that we will return home to Him.

Spirit

My heart goes where my feet walk,
My soul goes where my heart is.
My spirit goes where I am,
My voice goes where my heart sings,
My essence goes where my heart loves.
Spirit am I, spirit am I,
Seeking, seeking, seeking.
Spirit am I, spirit am I,
Knowing, knowing, knowing.
Spirit am I, spirit am I.

Chapter 36

Illusion

You are explaining how you decorated your bedroom. Are you sure? Does it exist? Can you prove it exists? Yes, one can take a photo. The photo is only that which is present when or where you took the photo. Yes, you are describing it to me. Is it real or an illusion? The room exists in your thoughts. The room is created every time you enter it. It may be cluttered, yet our minds are powerful enough to create it over and over again.

If this is an illusion, what is real? I don't know. Are we having an experience we created? If this is an illusion, then nothing matters. Does it? Does it matter if we are responsible in our thoughts and deeds? Is it okay to murder? Does it mean nothing because it is an illusion? Responsibility and actions are not the same as an illusion.

We are spirits with physical experiences. We are to learn, grow, and evolve in spirituality. This illusion of this world we create is the place for our evolvement. What is the goal? To create heaven on earth!

"Do I love thee?
With all my might.
Do I know thee?
With all my heart.
Do I hold thee?
With all my soul."
—Berdee, green parakeet

Chapter 37

To and Fro

"Uh!" Arline said frequently when she lifted her hand, shrugged her right shoulder, and slightly tipped her head in the direction of her open hand. It was her way of saying life is as it is. The gesture tickled my belly whenever she did it.

I met Arline at Sunday Celebration and on Monday evenings for A Course in Miracles (ACIM). Arline is known in the community as the chocolate lady. She makes delectable and creative chocolates for special events. Arline's sophistication exudes personality. She is older than me and is confident about her age and her life. This is something I admire. Should we not enjoy the special attainment of years and moments of a life lived fully?

Arline is Jewish and devoted to synagogue. She comes to our Sunday Celebration, feeling the enjoyment of the spiritually minded people, environment, and the land surrounding the celebration service. She often expresses the wonderful feeling she receives being with others who are working on their spiritual journeys as she seeks hers. She is interested in others, is an attentive listener, and helps when asked. She frequently asks me questions to better understand her journey in this time and place.

After the ACIM gathering or Sunday Celebration, Arline asked questions if there was something she was struggling to understand. She openly expressed inner conflicts that I knew the answer to that which she was seeking. She was grateful for my response, and I was grateful for her existence in my life. Arline gave me the beauty of sharing and trusting each other.

After Sunday Celebration, the people who attended would go out for lunch. It was sometimes difficult for the restaurants to handle so many people. We made sure to let the restaurant know we were coming.

This time we met at a family restaurant that specialized in seafood. Arline sat across from me and reminisced about her father. He was an exceptional magician, and her eyes danced as she talked about him. He was always doing magic tricks. Her father lived in the time of Houdini and knew him. Houdini came from my familiar stomping grounds of Appleton, Wisconsin. According to Arline, her father's magic tricks were on par with the great magician. She acknowledged that Houdini was more famous than her father. I quietly sipped hot coffee, nodded eagerly, and listened to every word of her memories. Her close relationship with her father was still strong in her heart.

Arline pursed her lips, and I anticipated a question. Arline had a dream for years and was unable to figure out what it meant. She had asked a lot of people about it over the years. She asked me to help her understand because no one else had been able to give her the answer.

In her dream, she was outside in her backyard in a hammock. The weather was comfortably pleasant and peaceful. She was enjoying the sun's warm glow on her face. She gently rocked in the hammock, feeling the slight breeze as the leaves rustled in the trees above her. She glanced toward the back of her home and noticed a man on a ladder washing her large picture window. When the man turned and smiled, she realized it was Jesus.

The restaurant was a bustle of chatter, and I moved in closer to her. I knew the answer was simple, and I wanted her to hear every word I spoke. "Clear vision," I said.

She slumped back in her chair and understood the true message in those two words. Clear vision was an amazing insight into Arline's spiritual quest to be open.

ACIM was a gift from Yeshua so we may move forward in our understanding and spiritual growth. Arline was open to understanding and living a spiritual life. She attended ACIM to seek answers to live spiritually. She continued to attend synagogue. People attend service to grow spiritually while remaining in the formal church/temple they grew up in. Fear holds them back from the freedom of feeling their independent spirituality. The spiritual place they seek is often called a *bridge church*. Bridge churches will not exist when we become spiritual in unity.

Arline's open heart accepted her synagogue and the teaching of Yeshua. Both gave her great comfort. My mind raced forward. When a window is washed, does it allow the light to enter and spill forth into the heart of the home? Clear vision was Arline's quest for truth and opened her heart to the light of awareness. The washed window represented her heart opening to the light of expanding inner spirituality, inner truth, wisdom, and connection to the divine within her. Arline's dream gave her insights into the changes within her.

The spiritual church, Divine Heart, is for the Second Coming of Yeshua. Yeshua named the church "Divine Heart." Yeshua ben Joseph is Hebrew. Yeshua is Aramaic. Jesus is Greek. Lord Sananda is His spirit name. The first time, He came for us all, which Arline often acknowledged. She was interested in the events taking place in our lives regarding Yeshua.

Arline's joy awakened the miracle of divine harmony and true vision. Her spontaneous humor and joy filled my heart with abundant laughter.

"Where did I go? Not far,
Was I lost? Yet found.
Where did I go? Not far,
Where was I? Not far.
Seeking the world nearby,
Seeking the world,
Learning the world,
Returned to love hereby."
—Bucko, cat

Chapter 38

A Different Drumming

I am myself. I am not a crowd or trend follower. Some call being true to oneself being different in a negative way, weird, crazy, and so it goes. What would this world be without its differences? Where would the artists, songwriters, singers, poets, and creative endeavors be without differences? It is only seeing or being in a creative expression.

Do I want to be one fish in a school? Following the crowd may have benefits when it is for charity or for pitching in to help someone. An elder said, "One hand washes the other." The Bible states, "Do unto others."

When we see differences in others or their beliefs, we are creating separation and division. Unity is the web of knowing we are One. There is a connection, yet there is freedom of choice for different expressions or experiences.

"My tears are for the love of our Lord.
Tears are the liquid of the soul."
—Betsy, a Camel

"Swirls of colored leaves,
Rustle the ground,
A farmer turns them into a mound.
My feet kick up orange,
Yellow and red,
Swirls of colors fly up in the air.
Onto my head,
Swirling into a twister,
And landing gently to bed."
—Elf, Lhasa Apso

Chapter 39

Winter Heart

Thump! The pine log landed in the middle of the fire, and sparks flew from the red embers. A petite woman with graying brown hair and blue eyes was stoking the fire as it danced to an unknown tune. On the mantel of the fieldstone fireplace, red tapers and white tea lights glowed. On the mantel, there was a lacy card with a red foil heart scripted with the word *love*. Inside the card, there was an ode to a Valentine sentiment. Behind the card, a milk glass vase held a single pink rose.

The woman walked toward the bedroom and emerged with a wedding ring quilt and one pillow in her arms. She dropped the quilt and the pillow on the floor in the family room between the coffee table and the fireplace. The antique pine rocker next to the coffee table embraced a blue floral seat cushion upon which a black and white cat was sleeping.

The coffee table was decorated with a vase of peppermint carnations with a red column candle in the middle. The flame of the candle filled the room with an apple-cinnamon fragrance and mingled with the smoke in the cozy room. On a wood tray, there were two bottles of Milwaukee-brewed beer and a bottle opener. Next to the wood tray, there was a round pewter plate with sesame crackers, deer summer sausage, and Colby cheese. Next to both trays were white paper napkins imprinted with pink and red hearts in different sizes.

On the floor next to the coffee table are two boxes; the one with tissue was empty. The other box holds a folded long, white silky nightgown with small red hearts on the bodice and a narrow red satin ribbon tied in a bow. Alongside the nightgown is a bottle of rose-scented perfume. The box and gown shared the lingering fragrance of rose perfume.

Humming to the radio's soft music, the woman, wearing slippers, scuffed past the fireplace to the bay window. She leaned forward to place her hands on the windowsill. A moment later, she stood upright and crossed her arms over her bulky red sweater dotted with tiny white hearts. Her crossed arms gave a sweater hug to hold in the warmth against the chill of the night. Her wool skirt is plain red, and she wears pink, fuzzy furry slippers.

Outside the wind of a Midwest blizzard is howling like a lone wolf. The woman felt the cold snap through the double-paned glass window. The streetlight illuminated the snowflakes swirling in the darkness. The icicles on the eaves appear lit from within. In the distance, a train's whistle declared its journey down the tracks. She would prefer a clear midnight black sky and the beauty of the northern aurora borealis. She knows God gives each night its own blessed beauty, and tonight it is the snowstorm.

Her head tipped to the intermittent sound of metal scraping against the cement sidewalk that leads to the garage. He is shoveling snow and will probably shovel again before sunrise. Snow is very heavy to shovel if left to accumulate and pack itself down. The sound of shoveling stopped, and she could hear him stomping the snow off his boots on the back porch. A long leather strap of sleigh bells jingled to announce his entrance. She shivered as he opened the back door, bringing the crisp cold freshness of winter in with him. Bundled warm, his brown down jacket rustled as he removed his knitted gloves, scarf, and stocking cap. Each boot thumped as it landed on the linoleum floor.

His footsteps stopped behind her as she stood in front of the window. His arms surrounded her waist. She covered his cold hands with her sweater and winced as his cold hands chilled her bare belly. His cheek was icy against hers, and she raised her palm to cover his other cheek and warm it. Nuzzling, his frosty nose breathed warm air against her neck.

The feminine urge spilled forth as she turned to face him. She pulled down the neck of his T-shirt and kissed the soft spot at the base of his throat. He was wearing his red plaid flannel shirt, a gift from her. The shirt was infused with his manly scent. He was an earthy man, big and gentle. They turned to sit on the floor between the coffee table and the crackling fire. He reached for the quilt and enveloped her.

He opened a bottle of beer, and she smiled as he sucked on the glass bottle. It reminded her of their baby suckling at her breast. His lips moistened her fingers as she fed him small bites of sausage and cheese. Between each bite, she unbuttoned a button of his shirt. The music on the stereo changed to country music, and she sang along to "I Wanna Dance" by Eddie Rabbitt and Billy Joe Walker.

A soft giggle emerged from her throat as their eyes shared the soul of each other. Her breath hesitated for a slight instant, and the tip of her tongue held her lips slightly apart. His hazel eyes held her face in a soft gaze. His eyes twinkled with golden sparkles of desire.

Morning Light

We danced in the morning light,
We danced, long before we knew,
Lips yet whisper the other's name.
Love dances, a new dawn arises,
In morning light, in dawn's soft light,
Awakened feathers sing His praise,
Melodies fill the morning air.
On navy nights, starlight wishes,
The man in the moon snoozes,
Dewdrops line the sleeping grass,
Slumber dreams now awaken.
In morning light, his arms embrace me,
Encircle our heart light within,
The moment pause, stops time.
Now holding me against his chest,
Feeling his heartbeat, love entwines.
In morning light, in dawn's soft light,
The breeze flutters from angel wings,
Our breath shares each other's soul.

Chapter 40

Candle Prayer

Candle Light is a prayer for animals and their guardians in need of healing, comfort, or guidance:

Divine Light within, we send our energy, love, and support as animals and guardians endure this time of crisis. Giving strength to their guardian families in providing comfort to their animals in this time of need. They are not alone during this time of worry, sadness, or mourning. We bless the animals for giving us their devotion and unconditional love. May we return our love, honor, and respect for them in our prayers. We hold animals in our hearts. They are true spirits—sentient and conscious of the Divine Light. May life be shared with joy, tears, and love between humanity and all creation.

Acknowledgments

TO:

Father God for each moment He works through me.

Our Blessed Mother who walks alongside of me.

Yeshua for His love envelops me.

Ascended master Sanat Kumara who filled me with his essence. With Him I experience the true feeling of incomprehensible peace.

The angels sent by God to protect us in our travels:
Jonathon, Thomas, David, Gabriel, Jonah and Gloria.

The archangels who are my protectors and guides: Uriel, Michael, Zadkiel, Raphiel and Gabriel

The higher light beings. David, who is present in my sessions with people. Sarah, who is present in my sessions with animals. Thank you for allowing me to give you names.

My primary spirit guides: Andrea, St. Anthony, Anetonka, and the Chosen Many.

Michelangelo who is my channel for portrait sculpting the Chosen Many.

The League of Women: women from my present and past lives unite in spirit to guide my journey in accomplishing my tasks from God.

The many I have learned from over the years: Anita Curtis, Dawn Hayman, Sandra Ingerman, Karen Peters, Dana Robinson, and Penelope Smith. And many, many others physically or in spirit, authors, including the Chosen Many, who left their imprint in moving me forward spiritually.

All creatures, this earth, the four elements, the universe.

My husband and office manager, Henry, for his energetic support, patience, insight, knowledge, and companionship. With his ability to edit he became affectionately called my "correctional officer."

Those who trusted my communication with their loved ones on earth and in spirit.

Balboa Press and staff, my kindest thoughts and exuberant thank you for their support, patience, and guidance. It was my dream to write and with your steadfast enthusiasm this book became a reality.

Credits

Front Cover
Thinkstock: Getty Images
Collection: Hemura
Artist: Konstatin Kalishko
Eagle Owl
Photographer: pigphoto

Back Cover
Thinkstock: Getty Images
Collection: iStock
Artist: R. E. Leon

Executive Portrait: Karen Kober
Gene Paltrineri Photography
Dover, NH 03820

NOTES

Printed in the United States
By Bookmasters